"You hold in your hands a true story of journey of a committed couple who hear terminal cancer.' In this vivid account, w mother as she struggles with grief, loss, an... of us who know Margaret, along with the thousands who followed her daily blog, can assure you that in the midst of tears you will be encouraged with words of hope, comfort, and the assurance that we shall all meet again in the presence of Jesus. Do yourself a favor and read this book, and then share it with a friend! Here, through the lens of a Christian woman, we learn that cancer does not have the last word!"

—Dr. Erwin and Rebecca Lutzer
Dr. Erwin Lutzer is Senior Pastor, Moody Church, Chicago

"In a careful blending of tenderness and tears, humor and cold facts, Margaret Nyman gives us a remarkable book of 'widow wisdom' that is insightful and practical. I have read dozens of books on handling grief, and even wrote a couple myself, but I assure you that this book is at the top of my list. If you need comfort for yourself or help in comforting others, *Hope for an Aching Heart* is a treasury you will not exhaust."

—Warren W. Wiersbe
Author and former pastor, Moody Church, Chicago

"Margaret Nyman is gut-wrenchingly real about the struggles she endured in the wake of her husband's death, just six weeks after he was diagnosed with pancreatic cancer. It is a journey she never would have chosen for herself. But in the midst of deep grief, she has experienced an even deeper awareness of Christ's presence and the comfort to be found in His promises. These short, poignant devotionals will minister grace to widows in every stage of the grieving process. They will also speak to all women, married or single, about how to reach out to widows in meaningful ways, and about trusting the Father's heart in every season of need and distress."

—Nancy Leigh DeMoss
Author and *Revive Our Hearts* radio host

"Margaret's book is a must-read for every widow. I wish I had *Hope for an Aching Heart* when I began my journey alone. It's personal, like she's walking beside us through our ordinary, daily events. It's important because we desperately need wisdom and comfort, and her extraordinary insights deliver both."

—Miriam Neff
Author, *From One Widow to Another: Conversations on the New You*

"Margaret Nyman is an accomplished artist and talented writer, but her greater gifts lie in her marvelous sense of hospitality, empathy for others, and wisdom gained as a wife, mom, and grandmother. As you read her book, you will benefit from her experiences, her observations, and her insightful life lessons."

—Dr. Dennis E. Hensley
Author, *The Power of Positive Productivity*

"Margaret Nyman shares her heart as she and her family lived through the unexpected death of her husband, Nate. Her words speak courage and humility. Grief cannot be medicated. The book urges patience and trust. Waiting is so difficult, and yet Psalm 23:4 guarantees that we are never alone. The Lord is with us."

—Dr. George Sweeting
Chancellor Emeritus, Moody Bible Institute, Chicago

"What you will find in these pages is a companion who invites you to walk closely with Jesus as you grieve the loss of a loved one . . . Readers will find encouragement, solidarity, and joy for the days ahead as they rest in Jesus through the words of Margaret's daily invitations. Thank you, Margaret, for an important gift that we can pass on to others who experience the loss of a spouse and loved one."

—Kyle and Lindsay Small
Co-pastors, Harbert Community Church, Sawyer, MI

"Like a crushed rose that produces a beautiful perfume, Margaret Nyman's journey through sorrow and loss has produced a poise and peace that honors Christ and draws others who want to know more of Him. This beauty is reflected in her writing, which exudes the fragrance of genuine faith in the harshest realities of life. This is a book to savor as you look to the Lord, who is able to bring beauty from ashes."

—Colin S. Smith
Senior Pastor, The Orchard, Arlington Heights, IL

Uplifting Devotions for Widows

Hope *for an* Aching Heart

MARGARET NYMAN

DISCOVERY HOUSE
PUBLISHERS®

Hope for an Aching Heart: Uplifting Devotions for Widows

© 2012 by Margaret Nyman

Discovery House is affiliated with RBC Ministries, Grand Rapids, Michigan.

Requests for permission to quote from this book should be directed to: Permissions Department, Discovery House Publishers, P.O. Box 3566, Grand Rapids, MI 49501, or contact us by e-mail at permissionsdept@dhp.org

ISBN: 978-1-57293-568-6

Interior design by Michelle Espinoza

Library of Congress Cataloging-in-Publication Data

Nyman, Margaret.
Hope for an aching heart : uplifting devotions for widows / Margaret Nyman.
    p. cm.
  ISBN 978-1-57293-568-6
1. Widows—Prayers and devotions. I. Title.
  BV4908.N96 2012
  242'.4—dc23   2012016401

Printed in the United States of America

Second printing in 2013

In loving memory of my husband, Nate.

God blesses those who patiently endure testing and temptation.
Afterward they will receive the crown of life that God
has promised to those who love him.

James 1:12 (NLT)

Contents

Part 6: Moving Forward

Introduction

My husband, Nate, passed away after only forty-two days of warning. Although pancreatic cancer won the earthly battle for his body, his soul slipped away to paradise unharmed, secure in Christ's victory over death.

Nate died at home, encircled by our seven adult children, two in-law children, my sister, and me, allowing us the holy privilege of seeing him off as he stepped into eternity. To know he left his cancer in the bed and received perfect health one moment later was cause for celebration.

But in those moments immediately after he died, the eleven of us stood around his bed sobbing and passing the tissue box back and forth over him, wondering what to do next. In an instant his life had changed for the good, but ours had changed for the bad. That night we couldn't know the extent of the changes coming, but in the two years since, every life category has been altered because of his absence.

God tells us in Scripture that He "lifts those bent beneath their loads" (Psalm 145:14 NLT). After a husband dies, his widow becomes pinned down under a load of grief. For me, the words "I can't" pounded me into a puddle of tears beginning with "I can't believe I'm a widow." My new situation laid a load on me far heavier than I thought I could bear, and you may feel the same way. But the book in your hands offers proof that God does, indeed, do the heavy lifting for a widow.

These sixty devotionals will help you move from shock to stability. As you read one each day, you'll gradually realize God is steadily lightening the burden of your new role as a widow, encouraging you to keep moving forward.

I'm praying for you.

Margaret

Part 1

I Can't Believe I'm a Widow

1

Why Ask Why?

Many times each day I walk past the little room in my cottage where Nate's hospital bed used to be, the place where he lay hovering between life and death for three days. Despite the exhaustion and stress of that time, sometimes I wish we were back there watching and waiting. If we were, Nate would still be with us.

I've never asked God why He let Nate die, because God doesn't usually answer our "why" questions anyway. Even Jesus, hanging on the cross in agony and asking why, didn't get His answer. When calamity comes, God has either caused it or allowed it, and He has significant reasons behind the whys. He just doesn't share them with us.

As the family faced planning Nate's funeral, my son Nelson and I sat at the dining table early in the morning. Although there was much to do, we decided to take a few minutes to think, talk, and pray. When I had entered the room, Nelson was reading the Bible story of Jesus calling to the disciples from the beach. The men had been out fishing overnight without success and were coming in, still one hundred yards offshore.

Jesus yelled for them to throw their net out once more. Without questioning Him, they did it and caught 153 large fish (John 21:11). As they happily dragged the massive catch toward shore, they saw Jesus standing by a fire and smelled the food He was cooking. What a breakfast of blessing this must have been for these hardworking men.

Nelson said, "They'd fished all night without success. Then Jesus asked them to do something that didn't make any sense. What difference could one more toss of the net make? But they did it." From the story, we know their obedience paid off handsomely.

Nelson and I talked about how life would be radically different without Nate. By allowing his death, God was asking us to do a new thing that made no sense to us. He wanted us to think and act differently from that point on. When Jesus shouted His fishing idea to the disciples, they didn't shout back, "Why?" Against all human logic they threw their net over the side. We didn't ask why about Nate, either.

Nelson and I decided that morning we'd follow God and do whatever He asked, which was to live life without Nate. Although we saw no blessing in that, we chose to believe God would surprise us, just as He did the fishermen.

> *[Jesus] said, "Throw your net . . . and you will find some [fish]."*
> *When they did, they were unable to haul the net in*
> *because of the large number of fish.*
> John 21:6

Lord, I crave answers, but you don't always give them. Help me to accept your ways, knowing there will be blessing coming through them. Amen.

2

The Widow Word

I remember when the word *widow* first entered my mind. It was just a few days before Nate and I were told he had terminal cancer. I was sitting in a warm bathtub in the early morning hours after Nate had had a bad night with intense back pain. He was finally asleep, and I grabbed the chance to decompress behind a closed door.

The tub wasn't even full before I was weeping, panicking at the unknowns in our immediate future. We knew Nate had a "mass" on his liver. What if it was cancer? What if he died? What if I became a widow?

Because we'd recently moved 110 miles from my sister, my girlfriends, my prayer groups, and my church, I panicked. But God, the tender Father, interrupted that downward spiral by flooding my mind with names, friends who would come if I asked, women who were faithful to God and also to me. These names equated to good future counsel and shoulders to cry on.

When I climbed out of the tub, I felt much better than when I'd climbed in, even though the facts hadn't changed. God had spoken to my need, demonstrating again how close He was. Psalm 116:2 pictures Him bending down to listen or turning His ear toward us, both intimate pictures of His tender care. Knowing He's aware of our emotional condition at any given moment is an ongoing comfort.

My focus, and also that of Nate and I as a couple, had been riveted on health issues for many weeks, but God knew precisely when my meltdown would occur, and He was ready. I've learned He is practical and rushes toward us with exacting sufficiency. As a doctor matches drugs to a patient's illness, so God matches aid to His children's crises.

When I was in the tub, submerged in despair, the Lord supplied a mental list of caring friends. I didn't head for a bath thinking, "Maybe God will help me there!" No, He just saw my tears, knew perfectly how to help, and did so. I believe He experiences delight in ministering to our needs, never running out of creative ways to do it. Surely new crises are ahead, but He's met me in so many emergencies that I don't doubt He always will.

As for my God-inspired group of women supporters, when I thought about each name, I realized how thorough His help really had been. Every single person on the list was a widow.

Such is the confidence that we have through Christ toward God.
Not that we are sufficient in ourselves to claim anything
as coming from us, but our sufficiency is from God.
2 Corinthians 3:4–5 (ESV)

Lord, prepare me for whatever is coming, and when it gets here, show me what to do. Amen.

3

Planning a Funeral

Within forty-eight hours of Nate's death, each person in the family had experienced the phenomenon common to every griever. We expected Nate to walk in the room momentarily or were sure we'd heard his voice, his laugh. Even at the store as I paid for the black suit I'd wear to his funeral I thought, "Nate will like this."

The mourning process is forced on us even before death's reality has sunk in. One minute we remember, the next we don't. Each disappointing "oh—that's right . . ." brings a wave of nausea, and then, in the midst of this misery, we have to plan a funeral.

All of us remember our first experience with death, maybe a grandparent or great aunt. We may have seen an adult cry for the first time. We sensed our parents setting us aside for more serious matters. The subdued atmosphere of the funeral home made us uncomfortable and anxious to leave.

But this time our assignment was to *plan* the funeral, not for a distant relative, but for a husband, a father. How could we?

We started with questions. What should be said? What sung? By whom? What part should family members have? Who will write the eulogy? Who will read it? What about pictures? How displayed? And flowers? What type? What cost? What about an obituary? Which papers? How should we act? What will we be expected to say? Who will come? What will we wear? And most excruciating of all, how will we choose what this man will wear in his own casket?

It's like trying to plan a wedding in three days, and of course there's no new beginning at the end of it. Instead, it's all about finishing. The finality of death pounds like a sledgehammer: he's gone, he's gone, he's gone.

But our family had no choice. Just as we dealt with the violent blows of Nate's cancer together and shared the agony of his dying moments, we stepped collectively into planning his funeral. Despite the necessary focus on his death, God led us to also discuss his new life. He'd been plucked from physical suffering and been given a pain-free existence with Christ.

We believe the Bible and therefore had to agree that coming face-to-face with Jesus in a new, joyful reality was better than anything this life could offer. Nate was "away from the body and at home with the Lord" (2 Corinthians 5:8). Being happy for him somehow brought comfort to us.

And his funeral, it turned out, was the celebration of a new beginning after all.

The Spirit of the Sovereign Lord [will] . . . bestow on them
a crown of beauty instead of ashes, the oil of joy instead of
mourning, and a garment of praise instead of a spirit of despair.
Isaiah 61:1, 3

Lord, when I lean into despair, pull me back by your Spirit and give me joy. Amen.

4

He's Unavailable

Shortly after Nate died, my son Lars struck a deal with AT&T. He persuaded them to shut down Nate's cell phone without a fee, even though we were breaking the contract. Where Nate is, he doesn't need a phone—a good thing for him but not so good for his family. We twelve were the people Nate loved most in all the world, yet none of us had any access to him. Our problem was that phrase, "in all the world." He'd left our world for another.

Scripture tells us, "We have a building from God, an eternal house in heaven, not built by human hands," guaranteed by the Holy Spirit (2 Corinthians 5:1–5). I was happy for Nate's new life there, but being so thoroughly separated from him in this world was difficult to accept. Holding his phone in my hand made that separation painfully real.

Three weeks after he died, I decided to check his messages and texts as a way to reconnect with my missing husband, although it felt like an invasion of his privacy. We'd always trusted each other, never opening one another's mail, checking on whereabouts, or monitoring phones. But I pushed past the "never," charged the battery, and brought up his voice mail.

One after another, callers expressed shock at his cancer diagnosis and offered to help "in any way." Many ended with "I love you." When Nate was sick, he found encouragement in these voices, and as I listened, they comforted me, too. Those callers will never know how valuable their short messages were to both of us.

After listening, I moved on to texts, a much harder task. Seeing the words on that tiny screen triggered something inside of me, and I started to weep:

"I'm thinking of you today and am sending my love."

"I'm here to talk whenever you want."

"We miss you very much and hope you can come back to work."

"I hear things are pretty rough for you and I am praying you will get relief from your pain."

"I just want to tell you again how very much your friendship is appreciated."

"I appreciate you so much for all you do and for how gracious you are."

"Please hang in there! We are praying very hard for you."

Suddenly I had an overpowering longing to send a message to Nate, and knowing I couldn't was excruciating.

The last text, sent the day he died, was, "Sending best wishes and prayers your way, and hoping you have a good day." That day did turn out to be good, actually spectacular, since Nate took up residence in heaven before the end of it. But oh how I miss him.

> *If anyone is in Christ, the new creation has come:*
> *The old has gone, the new is here!*
> 2 Corinthians 5:17

Lord, I miss my husband terribly but choose to thank you for his life. Because he's with you, he needs nothing more. Amen.

5

Two Good Gifts

Man's best friend may turn out to be woman's best friend, too. A few weeks after Nate died, several of us walked to the beach at sunset. The sky was spectacular with unusual brilliance for wintertime and was the perfect background for silhouette photos. It was during the picture-taking process I had my first experience of feeling like a fifth wheel.

My son and daughter-in-law posed for one picture; my daughter and son-in-law for another. Toddler cousins got together for a third. And then there was me, newly incomplete. My dog, Jack, was the best I could do.

Jack had been a true-blue pal throughout Nate's ordeal with pancreatic cancer. The day we first heard the dreadful diagnosis, Nate was not yet able to talk about it and had escaped into sleep. As I sat quietly trying to absorb all we'd been told by a team of doctors that afternoon, the finality of his diagnosis overwhelmed me. There was no cure, no treatment to slow the cancer, and no way to avoid death. I found myself swamped by wrenching sobs of sorrow, my hands covering my face.

Jack quietly walked to my chair and whimpered. I looked down and found him gazing up at me, lovingly coming to my aid. His whimper might simply have been a take-me-on-a-walk request, but I chose to think he was concerned about me. I slid to the floor, put my arms around his thick neck, and boohooed like a woman without hope, spilling tears all over his black fur.

A person can pour out his or her deepest hurts and fears to a pet with no inhibitions. Every secret, every doubt, every response to a crisis is safe with the animal. After a long, blubbering cry, I cupped my hands around Jack's handsome face and said, "If you could talk, I know you'd speak words of comfort to me."

Still looking directly into my eyes, he gave a little wag as if to say, "True." Even though nothing had changed about Nate, I felt much better.

The night of the sunset pictures, it occurred to me that soon all twelve family members would leave my home and return to their pre-cancer lives, and I would be living alone for the first time ever. I'd been with my parents and siblings, and then college roommates, apartment roommates, and finally Nate and the kids.

It seemed late to be starting something so radically new, but God reminded me of two good gifts: "You won't be living alone because you'll have Jack. And you'll have me."

The God of all grace, who called you to his eternal glory
in Christ, after you have suffered a little while, will himself
restore you and make you strong, firm and steadfast.
1 Peter 5:10

Lord, thank you that you're a Friend who understands even better than the most loving of pets. I'm so glad you'll never leave me. Amen.

6

Dressed for the Occasion

After Nate died, Sundays became the most difficult day of every week. First choice was to stay in bed under the comforter, hidden away in a safe place. Going to church meant putting together an outfit, a task I couldn't always accomplish.

In my confusion over why Sundays were so miserable, I decided to look up the stages of grief, wanting to know where I was and what was next. The seven stages are denial, pain, anger, depression, turning upward, reconstructing life, and acceptance.

After studying detailed descriptions of each stage, I concluded I had a toe in all of them. Stage one, denial, occurred when I expected Nate to walk in the front door with his empty coffee mug, singing, "Hel-lo-oh!" Stage two, pain, came in church while watching couples share hymnals or hold hands. Stage three, anger, was my confusion at wondering who I could blame, knowing it couldn't be God. He'd tenderly cared for our family throughout Nate's illness and afterward.

Stage four, depression, was the reason I wanted to stay in bed many mornings, and stage five, turning upward, was the peace I felt while walking outdoors with the dog. The sixth stage, reconstructing life, occurred when I wondered which box to check on a new form: Mrs., Miss, or Ms. And the last stage, acceptance, began happening as we looked through Nate's financial records to find what we needed.

Bouncing in and out of grief stages is what defines life for a new widow, reminding me of a childhood game called Fruit Basket Upset. Participants sat in chairs forming a circle around one person. When the person in the middle shouted, "Fruit basket upset!" everyone in the chairs jumped up and ran to a new chair. While they were colliding in the middle, pandemonium reigned. And that pandemonium is what grieving has been like for me.

Jesus is someone who operates completely outside the realm of confusion and disorder. When we go to Him with our grief, He makes sense of our chaotic thinking. I remember in Luke 8 how He came upon the mayhem caused by a demon-possessed, crazy man who had been screaming, cutting himself, rejecting clothes, and refusing to be subdued, even by chains. Jesus calmly solved each problem and brought sanity to the man and peace to those around him. He even prepared the man for worship and dressed him beforehand.

The Lord wants to do the same for us widows, bringing order to our confusion and calm to our emotional extremes. He offers Sundays as a special day to pull in close to Him. And He's even willing to help us choose our clothes.

You turned my wailing into dancing;
you removed my sackcloth and clothed me with joy.
Psalm 30:11

Lord, when the emotions of grief become chaotic, please wrap my life in your peace. Amen.

7

Trying to Remember

Nate was a man who enjoyed a regular routine. He would leave the office at the same moment every afternoon, climb on the same train, and drive from the station to our house within a minute or two of the same time every evening.

He also delighted in the same bedtime routine, and part of that was doing something for me. Knowing I liked to have water at my bedside, he'd fill a big glass and set it on my nightstand. When I saw him walking toward the bedroom with that glass, I'd always say, "Oh, you don't have to do that. I can get it."

But he'd say, "I *want* to do it."

After we learned of his cancer, he continued the water glass ritual. Our bedroom at the cottage was upstairs, and those fourteen steps became more and more difficult for him. Even after he should have been gripping the railing, he carried my water instead. I wept knowing it would soon end.

With my head on the pillow, I thought of how Nate's faithfulness mirrored God's, the One who never forgets to meet our needs. The biggest difference is that human frailty insists faithfulness eventually end, while divine help never does, not for a married couple and not for a widow. "You, Lord, are mighty, and your faithfulness surrounds you" (Psalm 89:8).

Nate began his bedtime routine earlier as the cancer wore him down. I'd climb on the bed with him each evening to read e-mails and cards until he fell asleep, and then I would go downstairs to continue the evening. When my bedtime came, I'd step quietly into our dark room and head for my nightstand, carefully feeling for the water glass. Without fail, it was there.

I remember the night I tiptoed in after midnight, comforted by Nate's deep breathing. I felt for my water, and for the first time in years, it wasn't there.

The next morning I thanked him for bringing my water each night, explaining how I felt for it in the dark, telling him that the glass represented his faithfulness to me. I didn't mention it hadn't been there the night before. Both of us knew his escalating pain and fatigue had permanently ended that part of his routine.

After that I tried to remember the water myself but never could. I still felt for it but then would remember and head back to the kitchen. Eventually, though, I learned the new routine, which erased a sweet reminder of Nate's loving care. Remembering the water glass was a mini-forgetting of him.

And for a widow, that's how it goes. Remembering, forgetting, remembering, forgetting.

We remember before our God and Father your work produced
by faith, your labor prompted by love, and your endurance
inspired by hope in our Lord Jesus Christ.
1 Thessalonians 1:3

Lord, help me to remember the blessings of my marriage, and teach me how to be a blessing to others. Amen.

Rearranging the Past

When someone we love dies, we spend a great deal of time looking back. If we've been at the bedside as death arrived, we go over and over those final minutes. Watching someone die is distressing and the memories can't be dismissed by a quick act of the will. Looking back feels like honoring the loved one who's passed away, which in turn helps the one who's still living.

I've gone over the hours and minutes leading up to Nate's death again and again, mentally combing through the details. Something in me longs to dwell there for a while longer, knowing eventually my heart will leave for good. Though my mind will remember the facts, the sadness will one day be gone.

I find myself wanting to rearrange those significant events and conversations like a chef wants to put a messy spice rack back in order. Of course I know reorganizing the past is fantasy, but how do I swap looking back for moving forward?

Lately my grieving seems more strenuous than in those days immediately after Nate died, as if a scab covering a wound has been pulled off and the injury must begin healing all over again. Experts tell us we are moving through the grieving process well when we stop reliving those last days and the death scene, replaying instead memories of the good times before the disease arrived.

Was I slipping backward?

When I sought God's counsel, He responded by bringing a verse to mind: "Wait for the Lord; be strong and take heart and wait for the Lord" (Psalm 27:14). He was saying, "Healing will come, and I'm going to tend to it. Please be patient."

Recently I had a dream that let me know where I am emotionally. It seemed like a movie, and Nate and I were both in it. We were hugging, and then both stepped back to look each other in the face while holding hands. We continued back-stepping, letting go, without making any effort to stop ourselves. Neither of us seemed frustrated or distressed as the gap widened. Eventually we stepped back so far, both of us dropped out of the scene entirely.

Though the dream upon awaking made me sad, it was a slice of real-time life. Reality tells me Nate is gone from my sight. Yet when I relive those last weeks, he seems vaguely visible again, as if I'm being blessed with a quick visit from him. I know God plans to help me step back from those days of sorrow just like in the dream, after grief has been spent. But for now, I'm content where I am.

> *Though he brings grief, he also shows compassion*
> *because of the greatness of his unfailing love. For he*
> *does not enjoy hurting people or causing them sorrow.*
> Lamentations 3:32–33 (NLT)

Lord, even though I'm not healed of my grief, I'll wait patiently, knowing you'll bring healing in your good time. Amen.

Without Insurance

Nate would have been appalled. Without realizing it, I had been running around without health insurance. I went over the handlebars on my bike and had a full head scan and twenty-one X-rays in the emergency room without coverage. Two weeks later, at my annual ob-gyn appointment, I found out about it when the receptionist said, "Did you know you don't have insurance?"

Two months prior I'd signed up for a policy with a new company (after several accumulated hours on hold) and pulled the insurance card from my purse to prove it. The woman stared at her computer, bringing up my accounts with my previous company and my new one, and concluded I was wrong and she was right. Apparently there was a three-week gap between the end of one and the beginning of the other.

Dumbfounded, my first thought was, "Nate would never have let this happen." Although I'd asked what seemed like hundreds of questions in the process of switching insurance, apparently I'd neglected the most important one: "When does it start?"

Becoming impatient, the receptionist said, "If you keep your appointment today, you'll have to pay for everything yourself." I'd waited three months to get in and needed a prescription renewal, so I agreed.

The doctor spent forty-five minutes with me, kindly taking time to ask questions about Nate and my new life without him. I left her office in a daze, mentally calculating the cost of my lengthy appointment. I walked right past the girl at the desk and out the door.

An hour later, my cell phone rang. "Did you leave without paying, after you promised you would?" the girl said, beyond irritated. "I need a credit card number immediately."

The charge was $432, a bill I would never have had to pay if Nate had been managing our insurance. Spending the next day on hold with the insurance company's telephone Muzak, I grew angry with myself for such a failure.

Scripture says, "Do not be quickly provoked in your spirit, for anger resides in the lap of fools" (Ecclesiastes 7:9). I knew that but was frustrated over my extreme incompetence. How many other expensive mistakes would I make before I learned to do everything Nate did? Was it even possible to learn all I needed to know?

We widows dip in and out of aggravation, disappointment, and gloom as we tackle new, unwelcome challenges. But God has called us into widowhood and will equip us to travel through it. I'm helped by thinking of myself as an apprentice on a new job. God is my all-knowing, infinitely patient Instructor, and He wants me to succeed.

And there's more good news. He'll never put any of us on hold.

> *The end of a matter is better than its beginning,*
> *and patience is better than pride.*
> Ecclesiastes 7:8

Lord, please train me to do everything Nate did, or lead me to others who are willing to help. Amen.

10

Chiseled in Granite

This morning I woke to the music of rain on my roof, thankful it wasn't one year earlier. On that day, a few hours after Nate's death, we were still reeling while struggling to plan his wake and funeral.

In remembering that chaotic time, I recall none of us gave a thought to a cemetery gravestone. As it turned out, that didn't get done for a year. Today, however, I followed the instructions given by the cemetery representative and e-mailed our choices to him, surprised at how difficult that chore turned out to be.

Nelson had sketched a rough drawing of the stone we wanted, adding Nate's name (and mine), along with dates. Having decided to match my father's family headstone nearby, selecting a design wasn't difficult. But it was very hard tapping out the text for the stone. I made one mistake after another, my shaky fingers acting like they'd never touched a keyboard.

Requesting names on a gravestone is serious business, origin of the expression "carved in stone" to represent permanency. Once the letters and numbers have been chiseled into granite, that's it.

I checked and rechecked my short e-mail, making endless corrections. Digging out the photo of Dad's family headstone, I studied it with new eyes and unexpectedly felt connected to the carved list of long-buried relatives. Except for my parents, I'd not met any of them.

Dad was only twelve when his father bought the plot of graves in 1911 for their twenty-month-old baby, who'd died of pneumonia. I remember him describing that sad wintertime funeral in the cemetery, after which Dad's parents had to suffer the additional pain of sketching out a gravestone for their little one.

Scripture says none of us are exempt from distressing times, and they can be part of our heavenly Father's plans for us. First Peter 5:6 says if we're willing to humble ourselves under God's hand, He'll creatively lift us up "in due time." I believe this means that at just the right moment He'll lift the sorrow from those who are grieving, because the next thing Peter says is, "Cast all your anxiety on him because he cares for you" (v. 7). But circumstances could get worse before they get better.

When Dad's baby brother died, that wasn't the end of their sadness. The mother, my grandmother, died fourteen months later, forcing Dad and his remaining family back to the cemetery, swamped with fresh grief as they buried her. Dad's father, a new widower, must have agonized as he requested his wife's name be carved into their headstone.

Right then God lifted a bit of my sorrow by giving me a new reason to be thankful: Nate didn't have to choose my headstone. Because of his incredible devotion, this task would have been nearly impossible for him. Widowhood isn't easy, but Nate becoming a widower would have been much worse.

Recently the Lord reminded me that carving names into granite will one day end. Scripture says the graves of those who believe in Jesus will burst open and give up their dead (1 Thessalonians 4:16). Believers will be united with Christ, which goes for Dad's family and also for Nate. The need for headstones and cemeteries will end as eternal life begins.

> *The dead in Christ will rise . . .*
> *We will be with the Lord forever.*
> 1 Thessalonians 4:16–17

Lord, please give me the courage to focus on eternal life rather than earthly death. Amen.

Part 2

Letting Myself Cry

11

Crying a River

Being a widow translates into thousands of tears, maybe millions. We can hold them back in public, but eventually the buildup spills over, and we're weeping again. During the forty-two days of Nate's cancer, many of the letters and cards we received quoted a fascinating verse from Psalm 56 detailing God's thoughts about crying: "You [Lord] keep track of all my sorrows. You have collected all my tears in your bottle" (verse 8 NLT).

I'm a visual person who appreciates the thousands of word pictures God has tucked into the Bible. A bottle full of tears is a potent image of God's nearness to anyone who is upset enough to cry.

I've thought about our family's crying over losing Nate, wondering if this verse could also be literal. Many would say, "That's nonsense." But God can do anything He wants. Even the tears that slide down our cheeks and are whisked away by an available sleeve could easily reappear in God's bottle, if He so desired.

If this verse is literal, what might that bottle look like? Because the word for it is singular in Scripture, surely it would have to be giant-sized! What could God possibly want with all those tears? They're salty, as all of us know, having caught them with our tongues when they ran past our mouths. They're also clear.

According to Revelation 22:1, heaven will have a river of life flowing from the throne of God, "as clear as crystal." Is it possible God plans to use our tears to supernaturally create this river?

Just when we become speechless over such a possibility, we get another inexplicable fact about the tears in his bottle, from the same verse: "You have recorded each one in your book."

Each one? Such detailed record-keeping is imponderable, but of course God is very good with numbers. He keeps track of all our sorrows and cares deeply about our suffering.

Recently I took fifteen minutes to sit and listen to God on this subject, hoping He'd give me more insight, which He did. He reminded me of a widow friend's statement about crying: "No one likes a weeping widow." I know what she meant. When a widow hits the one-year anniversary of her husband's death, people expect her grieving to be complete. But God's verse about the tear-filled bottle says, "There's no time limit on your grieving. I see your hurting heart and am counting your tears. I'll always take them from you and 'own them' myself."

Such tender understanding brought relief to my mind . . . and tears to my eyes.

> *The Lord Almighty . . . will swallow up death forever.*
> *The Sovereign Lord will wipe away the tears from all faces.*
> Isaiah 25:6, 8

Lord, thank you that my tears over missing my husband are precious to you. Amen.

12

Evicting Fear

As a young child, I was afraid of the dark. Not exactly the dark, but of what might be hidden in it. One night I cried with gusto from the upstairs bedroom, hollering for Dad to come and save me. When he appeared in the doorway, I wailed out my problem. "My closet has a big bear in it!" I said, pointing to the half-open door and the darkness inside.

Dad confidently walked toward the closet, telling me there was no bear in there. "I'll prove it to you," he said.

Although I wanted to believe him and he'd never lied to me before, I was trembling as he reached for the doorknob. Pulling the covers up to my eyes, I shouted, "Watch out!"

He bravely opened the door, reached into the darkness to pull the string to turn on the light, and said, "See? No bear."

Squinting from the safety of my twin bed, I visually inspected the closet. There were all my familiar dresses hanging on the clothes bar, but no bear. Dad was right, and because he'd shown me I had nothing to fear, I felt safe.

Several of my own children have gone through periods of fear, virtually always at night. As a two-year-old, Klaus wouldn't sleep in his room alone but insisted on bunking with six-year-old Linnea. Then, when Hans was three, he wanted to sleep holding hands with Klaus, who had grown into a fearless four-year-old.

Some of my widowed friends have struggled with fear too. Although most husbands would be no match for an intruder with a gun, wives feel secure sleeping next to them anyway. Once a mate has gone, imagination alone can be fear's invitation to rush in.

On several occasions since Nate died, fear has crept into my bedroom. Climbing onto the bed at night is still the loneliest moment of every day and sometimes produces dread. "Did I just hear something? Is someone coming?"

But what's a widow to do? She can get a big, protective dog, but far superior to that is calling on the One who sees well in the dark and has control over it. In 2 Timothy 1:7 we learn, "God has not given us a spirit of fear, but of power and of love and of a sound mind" (NKJV). Fear originates with Satan. When we're afraid, we can bring God into our mental scuffle. He'll replace anxiety with peace, exactly like my earthly Daddy did for me years ago.

Having confidence in God's presence is a definite help during fearful moments. Whether it's dark outside the windows or inside my emotions or both, being certain the Lord is with me is even better than owning a big, barking, snarling attack dog.

The Lord turns my darkness into light.
2 Samuel 22:29

Lord, when fear overwhelms me, please light my darkness with your presence. Amen.

13

Revisiting the Grave

Nate's funeral unfolded far too fast for me. Once the service began, time to talk to friends or even family was nonexistent. Afterward everyone was ushered quietly to their cars, and even at the cemetery each move was prescribed. Sitting in the center chair facing the casket, I knew I'd want to return to the gravesite soon.

Nine days later, I was there. Despite the curvy lanes between cemetery sections, Nate's grave was easy to find. Our family had come to that spot every Memorial Day for decades, sharing memories of the six relatives already buried there. We'd taught our kids to think of death as a conclusion to earthly life and not to fear it. Mom used to help them plant flowers around the big headstone saying, "Every day we're all one step closer to the grave. I can't wait, because then I'll be with Jesus."

As I stood next to Nate's grave in a chilly November wind, his death seemed incongruous. At my feet was a strip of fresh sod 4' x 9' and three urns of flowers on their sides. Was it possible my husband was buried beneath that grass, lying there in his new grey suit? Hadn't I just told him how good he looked in it when he wore it to work? Hadn't he been to court wearing it the day we learned of his cancer? How could he already be dead and buried in it?

I thought back to the most recent Memorial Day when the family had gathered on that exact spot, twenty-four of us. In one of the pictures taken that day, Nate was sharing a memory while standing over the place where he would be buried five months later. Now I stood there alone with evidence of death all around me.

My heart started to pound, "It can't be! It can't be!"

Shivering from the cold and runaway emotions, I hurried back to the car and started the engine for warmth. A CD came to life playing my favorite hymn, "To God Be the Glory":

Great things He has taught us. Great things He has done,

And great our rejoicing through Jesus the Son.

But purer and higher and greater will be

Our wonder, our transport, when Jesus we see.*

Suddenly it dawned on me that I sing the words in a future tense, "*when* Jesus we see." But Nate can sing them in present tense, "I see Jesus!"

I looked over at his grave and knew he wasn't really there. His grey suit was, wrapped around a cancer-ravaged body, but the real Nate was long gone. He'd been transported to the place of wonder described in the hymn, and the ugly reality of death had been gobbled up through victory in Christ.

> *The perishable has been clothed with the imperishable,*
> *and the mortal with immortality . . .*
> *Death has been swallowed up in victory.*
> 1 Corinthians 15:54

Lord, when I focus on death, flood my mind with thoughts of life in Christ. Amen.

---

* "To God Be the Glory," words by Fanny J. Crosby, music by William Howard Doane. Public domain.

14

Dreaming of Love

When my husband died, like all widows I was thrown into a whirlwind of grieving chaos. In Scripture such deep sorrow is described as "eyes dim with grief" (see Job 17:7; Psalm 88:9). My eyes couldn't see a positive future or any workable solutions to my countless new problems. My "dim eyes" wanted only to glance backward to look for Nate.

Often I thought I saw him or heard his laugh in the next room. I expected him to walk through the front door any minute. I looked for his car to pull in the driveway, and I was sure I saw him in public.

And I dreamed about him.

One night I had a dream so real, so stressful, it woke me with a pounding heart. In the dream I was part of a festive crowd milling about in a room full of conversation and laughter. Suddenly I spotted Nate! He was busy greeting people with his familiar handshake and didn't see me across the room.

Frantically pushing through the partygoers, I planted myself directly in front of him with anticipation on my face. He noticed me and responded with a hug, warm and familiar, but something odd was going on. Strangers seemed to have as much claim on him as I did. Quickly I was bumped to the side as others moved in for their handshakes and hugs.

Stumbling backward, I lost sight of him and felt an overpowering sense of emptiness. Then I saw him again, heading for the door. Shoving people aside, I raced to stop him. "Nate! Wait up!"

He turned and smiled, as he had moments earlier, but was devoid of reunion enthusiasm. I threw my arms around him, determined not to let go this time. He patted me on the back like a parent pats a child who's hurt as if to say, "It'll be OK." And just like a wounded child not ready to receive comfort, I began sobbing.

My real-life sobs woke me.

For several weeks I pondered the dream. Was it a picture of heaven? If so, where was Jesus? Apparently I'd been so consumed with seeking Nate, I hadn't even thought to look for the Lord. Eventually I asked God what He wanted me to learn from the dream. As is sometimes true, His response wasn't easy to hear.

Although He thoroughly understood my overpowering longing to be with my husband, He also knew that looking to Nate for my comfort wasn't going to bring it. The most effective way to relieve grieving pain would be to turn my "dim eyes" toward Him.

Hanging on to a departed Nate could never bring healing, but clinging to an ever-present God surely would.

> *Look to the Lord and his strength; seek his face always.*
> *Remember the wonders he has done.*
> Psalm 105:4–5

Lord, teach me how to cherish memories of my husband while looking to you for my comfort and healing. Amen.

15

Unexpected Tears

It was ten months after Nate died, and Jack was a walking flea circus. I'd fallen behind on regular treatments, thinking he was flea-free and could fight them on his own. But because his itching, scratching, licking, and nibbling had gotten severe, my daughter Louisa and I took him to the vet.

In addition to chiding us for leaving Jack unprotected, the doctor suggested we have him tested for Lyme disease. "We've seen a lot of that lately," he said, so we agreed. He asked us to wait in the lobby while a tech drew blood from poor Jack. When we reached the lobby, an unusual drama was unfolding.

A family of four was entering the office: mom, dad, sister, and brother. The boy, maybe twelve years old, came in last, carrying a fluffy white pillow with a big Siamese cat lying on it. Louisa leaned over and whispered, "Family outing to the vet?"

But in two minutes we understood. Their cat was very sick, and they'd come to put him to sleep. The mother stepped up to the receptionist's desk with several pill bottles in her hand. "We never opened these," she said. "Maybe you can donate them somewhere. We never . . . we couldn't . . . we didn't . . ." and then she burst into tears.

Her daughter hugged her while she wept, and the receptionist offered tissue. Then suddenly I was sobbing, too. Louisa turned and said, "But, Mom, it's not our cat."

My crying made no sense, but watching that family struggle against the wretchedness of death caused emotion to well up inside me and spill out in tears. It had to do with death's forced separation from those we love, and of course it had to do with Nate.

God created us to live forever. He meant it to occur in a perfect world without sorrow, and when death aborts life, something inside us goes askew. The drama in the vet's office and the one in our home ten months earlier both belong in that skewed world.

Will there ever be an end to our tears over death's apparent victory?

Jesus said, "Very truly I tell you, whoever hears my word and believes him who sent me has eternal life and will not be judged but has crossed over from death to life" (John 5:24).

God hasn't changed His mind about us living forever, but because we sinned, He needed to make an adjustment to His original plan. Now most of us will suffer through earthly death to gain eternal life. But if we do things God's way by entrusting our lives to His Son, then death simply becomes the passageway to a death-free life . . . exactly as He first intended.

In this death-free life, unexpected tears will never occur again (Revelation 21:4).

> *Weeping may stay for the night,*
> *but rejoicing comes in the morning.*
> Psalm 30:5

Lord, I'm glad you will one day abolish death and eliminate sorrow. Until then, I trust you to love me through my tears. Amen.

Leave Me Alone

I remember a sorrowful moment several months after Nate died, in the dead of a Michigan winter. While walking the dog on an icy night, I was shivering with the cold but also the misery of missing my husband. Passing a neighbor's house, I saw through the window that the family was entertaining. While standing in the road watching, suddenly I felt like Hans Christian Andersen's little match girl, lonely and excluded from the happy gathering inside.

A week later, different neighbors invited me to dinner, but I refused. This made no sense, since it was my chance to get "on the inside." But that's new widowhood, a hodgepodge of emotions that say, "I'm lonely, but leave me alone; I feel excluded, but don't include me."

Not too long after my forlorn experience in the road, I walked into a friend's kitchen, noticing a long dinner table set for a crowd. A big pot of stew simmered on the stove, and fresh bread lay on the counter. Watching my eyes take in the festive setup, my friend said, "Our small group is coming tonight." I nodded. Then, without hesitation, she filled a bowl with steaming stew and handed it to me. "Why don't you take this with you?"

Gratefully I accepted her gift and stepped into the cold night with my warm bowl, feeling included but without the pressure to meet new people or make small talk. It felt exactly right.

Part of the problem with widowhood is that others don't know how to help. Yet we widows don't make it easy on them with our erratic responses to their attempts. We repeatedly refuse invitations to the point of causing friends to think, "What's the use? She just wants to be alone."

They don't understand, but someone does. Jesus was the ultimate example of an outsider. Having been partnered with God more closely than any marriage could ever be, He suddenly was on His own. Surely He was lonely, being separated from heaven and feeling out of place on earth. He was divinity locked in human limitations, sinlessness surrounded by sinners. Yet he persevered and accomplished His goal: "Christ Jesus came into the world to save sinners" (1 Timothy 1:15).

What is a widow's goal? It's to cope with profound grief while adjusting to life as a single woman, two assignments that take months and often years. Jesus knows exactly how we feel and presents an invitation different from our neighbors and friends. He identifies with our suffering and doesn't ask for small talk. Silence is just fine. Tears, too. He just says, "Come to me" (see Matthew 11:28 and John 7:37).

As we live in the shadows trying to cope with our new reality, Jesus will patiently, lovingly draw us from the outside . . . in.

> *"I have loved you with an everlasting love;*
> *I have drawn you with unfailing kindness."*
> Jeremiah 31:3

Lord, when I'm pushing people away, please continue to hold me close to you. Amen.

Cracked

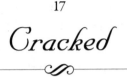

Our old, neglected asphalt driveway needed help when we bought the cottage eleven years ago, but driveways are low priority when home improvements begin. Recently, however, a man wearing tar-decorated clothes knocked on my door with an offer to make my drive look and stay beautiful. "I guarantee for three years," he said with confidence, handing me his card. We negotiated a price and set a day.

The asphalt expert arrived despite the threat of rain and brought along a tar-smudged partner: his wife. Never have I seen a woman spreading black goo on a driveway, but Diane added the attention to detail many men miss. She used a broom to spread the tar perfectly at the edges, taking care not to touch our concrete sidewalk or retaining wall.

The three of us became friends because we ended up spending more than the average driveway-tarring time together. Ten minutes after they finished, a cloudburst washed away much of their fresh work.

Diane and Charles returned two days later to assess the damage, and two days after that, they redid the whole job. Their good cheer impressed me as they worked just as carefully the second time, without any additional money.

When they finished my driveway for the second time, Charles pointed out something special. "See these cracks?" he asked. "I filled them with melted rubber, not tar. In three years that rubber will still be there, expanding and contracting with the seasons. It's tough stuff."

Later I wondered, what is a widow's "tough stuff"? Who does she call to fill the cracks left after her husband dies?

The answer can only be God. He has unlimited heart-and-soul filler, though He never spreads it into our lives without our permission. Scripture repeatedly reminds us He's ready with abundant joy to fill us up. He wants to pour good cheer into the ragged crevices of our broken hearts, pushing sorrow out as He flows in.

Paul reminds us that the living God "has shown kindness . . . and fills your hearts with joy" (Acts 14:17). Just like Charles and Diane's durable rubber fill, God's joy is the filler we widows need. It provides the give-and-take to weather ongoing storms and can stabilize the hot and cold of our frequent mood changes as we learn to live without our husbands. How do we take advantage of His supply? By calling on Him first, rather than as a last resort. We should detail our needs in prayer, and watch for the answers He provides.

When my driveway needs refurbishing, I'll call Charles. When my inner emptiness needs refilling, I'll call on God. Thankfully, He's always got more to give.

You will fill me with joy in your presence.
Psalm 16:11

Lord, my heart feels like it has cracked in two. Please come and fill my empty places with your joy. Amen.

18

Energizing Sleep

During the night God gave me a gift—ten hours of sleep. I can't remember ever sleeping that long, although as a teen I surely did.

Yesterday was strewn with meltdowns and tear-ups, and I've learned that grieving is exhausting. Although I didn't expend much physical energy, by the time I crawled into bed, I was whipped. Before Nate died, I had no idea about this part of widowhood.

Years ago I reached out to a newly widowed friend by inviting her over for lunch, just her and me. I knew enough not to include a crowd but had no understanding of her deep struggle. Without even pausing to consider my offer, she said, "Oh, I couldn't possibly. I don't have the energy."

Her response confused me, since I thought a simple lunch would be a safe place to share her grief. I didn't understand the drain it would be for her to choose the right clothes, get dressed, drive to my house, answer my questions, and maintain composure throughout her visit. Now, because I've walked in her shoes, her rejection of my invitation makes perfect sense.

All grief is strenuous, and not just on the body. Psalm 31:9 says, "I am in distress; my eyes grow weak with sorrow, my soul and body with grief." Losing a loved one knocks us flat for a while, body, soul, and spirit. And if our loss is a spouse, part of our identity has gone with him.

Although I've seen my parents die and experienced deep sadness both times, grieving Nate has been much worse. The parental bond doesn't have the same strength of two-becoming-one, a description of marriage. Since young couples are instructed to "leave [parents] and cleave [to each other]," husbands trump parents thereafter.

My sister, Mary, asked me yesterday if I missed Nate more than I expected. Definitely. One of the reasons is there seems to be no end to realizing the many ways he was dear to me. We were two halves of a whole, but when he was with me, I didn't give much thought to that. Now he's gone, and it's painfully evident. Without his half, I'm having a hard time standing.

Since none of us can walk in another's shoes until our experiences overlap, we can't appreciate someone else's response to a crisis, just as I couldn't know why my friend wouldn't come for lunch. Maybe that's why new widow friends have become precious to me. They've already walked the road I'm now on, and that validates their advice.

Many of them have counseled me to "get good rest." They were right. After last night's sweet sleep, today has been a much better day.

> *This is what the Lord Almighty, the God of Israel, says: ". . .*
> *I will refresh the weary and satisfy the faint." At this I awoke*
> *and looked around. My sleep had been pleasant to me.*
> Jeremiah 31:23–26

Lord, when I am depleted, please provide restful sleep. Amen.

19

Vinegar in a Wound

Suffering eventually comes to us all, which means we will eventually need comfort from others. Before my husband died, I had no idea how to console a grieving widow. After Nate's death, I realized many others didn't know either. Well-meaning comforters sometimes said the wrong things, not realizing every new widow is so stunned by what's happened that she's not yet ready to receive what they want to give. Even brief, thoughtful messages written inside beautiful sympathy cards are difficult to absorb.

A friend might write, "God will bring good from this," and the widow thinks, "How could God think taking my husband could be good?"

Another sympathizer might write, "The Lord is sovereign over your circumstances," and the widow thinks, "God could have saved his life, but He refused."

Though the intentions of friends are loving and the statements about God are true, a new widow can't make sense of them when her grief is raw. The same goes for social invitations: "May I come and visit you?" or "Shall we go out to eat?" or "Should we plan a getaway?" Nothing sounds good through a filter of excruciating emotional pain.

Scripture says, "Like vinegar poured on a wound, is one who sings songs to a heavy heart" (Proverbs 25:20). Even though words of comfort are meant to soothe, in the early days of widowhood many of them sting like vinegar.

As I opened the cards that came when Nate was sick and then after he died, I read the words but couldn't take them in. Instead I laid each one in a pretty basket in the living room, not knowing what else to do. Words of encouragement or even scriptural counsel couldn't "fix" me or speed up my healing, since mourning is a slow process that must occur step-by-step.

Timing is everything, and God is a pro at timing. He knows grief isn't a puzzle to be quickly solved or a hurdle to jump immediately. Instead He stands next to us until our torrent of tears lessens, knowing we'll hear His words better after that. He says, "As a mother comforts her child, so will I comfort you" (Isaiah 66:13), and just like a mom who instinctively knows what her children need, when the time is right, God soothes our tattered spirits.

We widows find our numbness gradually subsiding as time ticks by. Eventually I was drawn back to my basket of cards, needing and wanting to read them again. This time they provided the courage and strength the writers had first intended. The same messages that once felt like vinegar in a wound became a rich source of sustenance and comfort, building within me the will to move forward.

> *How abundant are the good things that you [Lord]*
> *have stored up for . . . those who take refuge in you.*
> Psalm 31:19

Lord, teach me how to accept the comfort offered by others and through it, to move forward. Amen.

20

Wrenching Impossibility

As a new widow, I often thought back to Nate's illness, reliving the events of those forty-two days. Our cottage was crowded with family, and when the atmosphere grew heavy with end-of-life issues, our toddler grandchildren cheered us with full-of-life antics. Toys were everywhere, symbols of happiness in a home laced with sorrow.

At fifteen months, little Skylar had discovered puzzles, amazing all of us with her expertise. She was especially good at one with tiny handles on each piece. Weeks after Nate had died and the family had gone, I washed all the toddler toys and put them away, readying them for the family's next visit. But sadly, Skylar's much loved puzzle had disappeared.

Months afterward, while cleaning in preparation for visitors, I was enthusiastically sweeping up clouds of Jack's dog hair, thinking how much better I felt compared to the year before. Back then, visitors meant stress. I felt resistance when trying to move a living room chair and reached underneath. There, wedged between the chair leg and the wall, was the lost puzzle. Like an unexpected electrical shock, a current of grief shot through me, because when that puzzle had slipped under there, Nate had still been alive.

Instantly I was shaking with an overpowering desire to go back to that day, not through memories, but for real. I absolutely had to be with Nate again! But of course that was a wrenching impossibility. Sobbing over a child's puzzle made no sense, but every widow understands this kind of eruption of grief. As I pictured him sitting in the chair above the puzzle, it was excruciating to have the toy but not have him.

Although circumstances differ, no one is exempt from the anguish of "wrenching impossibility." But God is the Master of possibility. Jesus told us so himself: "What is impossible with man is possible with God" (Luke 18:27). Although God *could* bring Nate back to me, it's more likely He'll bring new life into my widow-circumstances, strengthening me to wholeness through His promised help.

As I cried over Skylar's puzzle, my heart hurt, but gut instinct told me my outburst of crying was really a fresh burst of healing, a gift from God. He was gradually eliminating wrenching impossibility and bringing me closer to His gratifying new possibilities, tear by tear. This didn't mean other heartbreaking moments might not come, but making it through one more sorrowful episode strengthened me to make it through another.

Before I put the puzzle away, I studied it, picturing pudgy little hands at play rather than forlorn family members in the living room chairs a year before. And with that cheery mental picture, I could pick up my broom and continue sweeping.

I can do all this through him who gives me strength.
Philippians 4:13

Lord, when I'm longing for my husband, please eliminate wrenching impossibility and substitute the good healing that's possible because of you. Amen.

Part 3

Seeking a New Balance

21

Can I Help You?

Every one of us will eventually succumb to something. All of us will die. To be aware of death's approach is to receive a gift, even though at the time it may seem more like a curse.

When we've received a warning that death is on the way, it gives us a chance to say loving words to the one who will be leaving. We can also do our best to make wrongs right. Although in relationships we avoid blaming ourselves for anything, when a loved one is dying, we are quick to self-judge and genuinely want to do better.

During that first night after Nate and I learned a stage 4 cancer was growing rapidly within him, my mind flooded with regret. As he slept next to me in the deep fatigue of fatal disease, I lay in bed quietly weeping. Having always wanted to tweak this or that about him, I suddenly felt like a terrible wife. After forty years of marriage, I should have been long past such shallow thinking and far deeper into loving unconditionally. Even focusing on myself that first night instead of on him was an indication of my selfishness.

I prayed God would control my thinking as Nate and I embarked on what we thought would be a six-month journey. I asked, "What should I do about all my regrets, Lord?"

God answered me with a verse: "The Lord God said, 'It is not good for the man to be alone. I will make him a helper suitable for him'" (Genesis 2:18).

He was saying, "Stop looking back. Focus on today and simply help Nate. If you do that, you'll please him and also me." It was a massive relief to know He wasn't expecting me to be perfect, just helpful. That I could do.

If Nate was struggling to pick up something, I'd step forward with, "Let me help you with that." (Easy.) If he didn't have a drink next to his armchair, I went for ice water. (Easy.) If he had trouble with his shoes, I kneeled to wiggle them on. (Easy.) When doubt snuck in during the night telling me I wouldn't be able to handle Nate's ever-increasing needs, I cried out to God, "I can't do this!"

Then He'd gently calm me with, "Just help him."

When it was all over in six short weeks, being a helper had been all that was required of me. Why couldn't I have been a helper (not a manipulator or a controller) throughout our forty years together?

To this day, I still have regrets, but I continue to give them to God. I have determined to be a helper from here on out, and I know He'll help me with that.

> *We say with confidence,*
> *"The Lord is my helper; I will not be afraid."*
> Hebrews 13:6

Lord, thank you for promising to be my helper as I go about helping others. Thank you for never requiring more than I can give. Amen.

22

Grief Is Tricky

So far, I've had seventeen years as a child, four years as a college student, three years as a working single, and forty years as a married woman. Sadly, now I'll begin stockpiling years as a widow.

Two-thirds of my life has been spent thinking and acting like a wife. When I was a single career woman, I didn't feel awkward, but having been half of a couple most of my life, now I feel inept.

It's the little things.

For example, today I sent an anniversary card to dear friends. They're among the many couples Nate and I spent time with, always together in even numbers: four, six, ten. The hard part came in signing the anniversary card.

Although my head knows only my name should be there, the couple-words rolled out of my pen before I could stop them: "Love, Margaret and Nate." I looked at what I'd written and cried. Transitioning from being married to being single is rocky.

Another rough adjustment has been learning to talk about Nate in the past tense. I catch myself saying, "Nate loves banana cream pie," and then having to correct myself: "I mean, Nate loved banana cream pie." Using the past tense is painful enough to make the statement not worth saying at all.

A third issue has been receiving mail addressed to him. In the beginning, his familiar name on a utility bill or magazine gave me a flash-thought that he was still with me. Although the harsh truth rushed in immediately, for a split second he was back.

A grieving mind can play tricks that lean into fantasy: "If Nate is getting mail, that means whoever sent it doesn't know he has died, which leads me to believe there's a place where he's still alive, at least in someone's mind." Of course this is illogical, but that's how new widows think.

Thankfully we can be sure that as everything about our lives changes, God doesn't. As always, He's ready to help. Romans 12:2 says we can be transformed by the renewing of our minds, and He tells us how: "Be joyful in hope, patient in affliction, faithful in prayer" (verse 12).

When nothing else makes sense, God's instructions still do. He wants us to acknowledge that our many disconnects are simply natural stepping stones to a new identity. He'll patiently stick with us throughout the transformation. After all, the habits of forty years can't be changed in a day, or even a month. Maybe not even a year.

But as long as it takes, He'll be there to help.

> *Do not dwell on the past. See, I am doing a new thing!*
> *Now it springs up; do you not perceive it?*
> *I am making a way in the wilderness.*
> Isaiah 43:18–19

Lord, when I feel confused by the many changes I must make, remind me to trust in the new thing you're doing. Amen.

23

Will God Provide?

⟿

I don't feel like sixty-five, but that's the age the calendar tells me I am. Coming into widowhood during the same few months I came into Social Security made me nervous. Since we were a one-income family, I leaned on Nate for a household allowance and was happy to be in charge of only small amounts. Would I be able to manage money without Nate's guidance? What if I ran out and became a burden to my children?

I opened my Bible, craving reassurance from the One who owns all things. I read, "The Lord is near. Do not be anxious about anything" (Philippians 4:5–6). While I was concentrating on that, God brought an example to mind from years before when He'd provided in an unusual way.

Our family had suffered a financial setback, and I often stood in the checkout line at the grocery store with a cranky toddler on my hip and a near-empty purse over my shoulder. It's difficult to decide what items to take off the belt to bring a total below twelve dollars.

I became a pro at saving pennies and caring for leftovers by the pea and kernel of corn, and I don't mean from the serving bowls. Bits that were left on each plate were gathered to make one new serving for someone at the next meal. I learned to make soup, most often without meat, and we slurped it down, night after night.

During these stress-filled days, I began looking for God like never before, exactly like I am now, as a widow. I had to know if He saw the situation and how He might help. And then He let me "see" Him through what He did next.

On a bitter cold morning, I stepped out the front door to drive the school car pool. There, covered in sparkling frost, were two large paper grocery bags full of food: potatoes, oranges, cereal, butter, bread, canned vegetables, cookies, peanut butter, soup, and rice. Wedged into the bottom was a frozen ham.

The kids, leaning forward under the burden of school backpacks, tripped over each other to look into the bags. "Who? When? Why?" We never got the answers. But we all recognized God that day, and when He came, He taught us something important.

Although He lets us struggle in a variety of ways, including the death of our husbands, He's always watching out for us. I think He pays closer attention when we're experiencing pain than when things are going well.

On that discouraging winter day years ago, God loved us so much He leaned down from heaven and whispered into someone's ear: "Drop two bags of groceries on the Nymans' front porch today."

Or maybe He just did it himself.

> *My God will meet all your needs*
> *according to the riches of his glory in Christ Jesus.*
> Philippians 4:19

Lord, increase my trust in you and allow me to "see" you. Cause me to believe you wholeheartedly when you say you'll provide for me. Amen.

24

Creatures of Habit

Recently after leaving the local post office, I walked through the parking lot toward my car and without even thinking stopped at a white Chrysler minivan identical to one I owned two years back. My remote clicker wouldn't open it, of course, which let me know of my mistake. Although my red Highlander was the next car over, for a few seconds I was sure that "what used to be" was still true, that I still owned a minivan.

Most of us are creatures of habit. We find comfort in routine and enjoy regularity in our schedules. Some of us bristle at change. I've spoken with quite a few widows since Nate died, and no two stories are alike, but the one constant is disillusionment over the radical break from "the way we were." To be married several decades is to come into a period of marriage that is lovingly comfortable, and both husband and wife like it that way.

When death destroys that routine, happy habits are forcefully broken. Every life pattern changes. It's like flying in an airplane that's been on a straight course, when suddenly it begins doing loops, dives, and spirals.

Death wasn't God's idea, and He never intended that we'd have to adjust to its presence. Apparently He meant for Adam and Eve to continue forever in the perfection of Eden. But sinful choices deep-sixed that arrangement, bringing spiritual death immediately and physical death later. The Eden routine surely must have been a hard one to surrender. After all, Adam and Eve were forced to exchange their contented, carefree lives for blood, sweat, and tears.

The break from "the way they were" rearranged everything for Adam and Eve, including their home, their work, and their walk with God. Separation. Disconnection. Struggle. The changes must have been painful and required a long period of adjustment. But I'm sure the Lord encouraged them with a promise that still stands for us today: "Never will I leave you; never will I forsake you" (Hebrews 13:5). After their move from the garden of Eden, they were forced to develop new habits, and a different routine took the place of the old one.

Although old habits die hard, Adam and Eve did eventually adjust. And much to their joy and benefit, God stuck with them through the transition and beyond. He'll do the same for us today. As long as we live, change will yank us from our comfortable ruts, but fortunately, God has chosen to accompany us. We may view a husband's death as an airplane loop, dive, or spiral, a disturbing disruption of a familiar routine, but God will transform it into a fresh beginning.

He promises to stick with us, all the way.

> *Do not be afraid. Stand firm and you will see*
> *the deliverance the Lord will bring you.*
> Exodus 14:13

Lord, my husband and I loved our comfortable routine. Show me how to step out of it and embrace your new beginning. Amen.

25

A Fix for What's Broken

Cancer arrived only three months after we'd moved away from lifelong friends, church, and home. In a new state and new neighborhood, Nate and I had fully intended to begin putting down roots by finding a church, getting involved, and becoming acquainted with our neighbors. But disease forced us down a new path.

Nate died forty-two days after his diagnosis, and although our children and grandchildren stayed as long as they could, eventually they had to return to their regular lives. It was the dead of winter in Michigan, and I burrowed in at home, wanting only to stay warm and think of Nate.

About that time, my new neighbors began inviting me out. "Want to come for dinner? Does the church concert sound good? Could you use our extra banquet ticket? Or come for game night? Or join our book club?"

These kind invitations came when I was craving time alone, and I found reasons to say no to all of them. The one invitation I did accept turned into a fiasco because when the day came, I forgot to go. I called later to apologize but felt bad about it for weeks.

Being in public meant repeatedly having to answer the question, "How are you doing?" Holding back tears while being introduced as the woman who had "just lost her husband" was stress I couldn't handle for many months. All of it made my insides ache: making small talk, meeting new people, trying to smile.

I found comfort in a verse from the Old Testament that refers to Jesus: "He has sent me to bind up the brokenhearted" (Isaiah 61:1). I was glad God knew about my broken heart and was sure He understood I was falling apart because He used the words "bind up." Just as a well-wrapped sore limb feels better because of the bandage, His binding would be my firm support. The same passage says He'll comfort all who mourn and provide for those who grieve (verses 1–3).

Although it took many months, He was true to His word. Life began to get better. The ache, though still there, was quieter, and tears didn't come as quickly. Then one day, after a neighbor had repeatedly invited me to her Bible study without hearing a yes, I surprised myself by saying, "OK."

That study became my first away-from-home place of safety. All ages were represented among the women, and I learned many had walked into widowhood ahead of me. Each week, with Bibles on our laps, we talked of our sure hope in Christ. These women and God's Word became the binding for my broken heart, the provision for my mourning soul.

And with time, they became new friends in my new neighborhood.

All Scripture is inspired by God
and is useful to teach us what is true.
2 Timothy 3:16 (NLT)

Lord, show me the right balance between outings with others and at-home time with you. Amen.

26

Invisible Influence

My dog, Jack, and I try to walk to nearby Lake Michigan daily, year round. On summer days crowds abound, but during the winter, we have the beach to ourselves as far as the eye can see. When temperatures dip below thirty-two degrees, splashing waves gradually build heaps of ice fifteen to twenty feet tall, freezing solid so far from shore that not a sound can be heard on the beach.

We love climbing the ice-made hills, me sliding and stumbling while Jack and his claws scramble right to the top. The frozen mounds resemble mini-mountain ranges, complete with peaks and valleys, a breathtaking winter sight.

But their rock-solid appearance is deceiving. Though they look and feel firm, water moves beneath them, and calving could easily create icebergs, possibly leaving Jack and me wobbling on one of them. Surface cracks in the ice testify to the churning below, water that's freezing cold, hypothermia-inducing, and dangerous. Though invisible to my eyes, the lake water has the power to carve away at everything it touches with consequences that eventually become visible.

Much of life is about the churning of the invisible: our emotions, intentions, expectations. I'm inclined to believe the most critical parts of life are those moving beneath the surface.

God moves beneath the surface, too, and He uses His power in ways we can't see. But unlike churning water eating away at ice, His movement is for our benefit. For example, our invisible thoughts, the struggles in our minds, are visible to Him. The Bible says, "The secret things belong to the Lord our God" (Deuteronomy 29:29). This is good news for widows. It means He sees our mourning and wants to co-own it with us, sharing in our distress.

But how do we draw close to someone who's invisible to us? God knows it's difficult, so He has provided prayer as a way to feel closer to Him. When we talk to Him, He answers, and within those answers, we can "see" Him in the visible things and people He provides.

Though something is invisible, it doesn't mean it's unimportant. If I regularly walk on ice with water moving beneath it, eventually I'll be stranded on an iceberg. If I doubt God because I can't see Him, I'll eventually find myself drowning in a cold lake of emotional instability and sorrow, struggling to make it on my own.

A much better idea is to take advantage of His invisible influence for good in my life, and when I do, He'll let me "see" Him nearby, in visible ways.

You who fear the Lord, praise him! . . . For he has not despised
or scorned the suffering of the afflicted one; he has not hidden
his face from him but has listened to his cry for help.
Psalm 22:23–24

Lord, when I'm tempted to doubt your presence because I can't see you, please show me you're nearby. Amen.

27

Gummed Up

Although I graduated from a Christian college that demanded careful attention to academics, my friends and I never let studying get in the way of a good time. During our junior year we put together a country fair with baked goods, crafts, and games. When asked if I would host a contest booth, I told them the only special skill I had was blowing giant bubbles with bubble gum.

During the fair I sat in my stall next to a bowl of Bazooka bubble gum, selling chances to bubble-blowing challengers. Jocks, geeks, scholars, flunkies, faculty members, and even the dean of women squared off with me, but at the end of the fair, I remained triumphant. My bubble had always been bigger.

I still love bubble gum. My girls bought me a giant bucket of Double Bubble recently, and I quickly divided the pieces into baggies for my beach bag, the car, my dresser, and the kitchen cabinet. Sadly, though, my penchant for gum got the best of me. A dental bridge over a missing tooth broke lose while I was chewing.

A week later I was in my dentist's chair, explaining how the specific pain beneath one tooth had begun to throb and gradually spread over half my face. Campaigning for sympathy, I said, "Stabbing cheek pains woke me three times last night!"

He explained. "The tooth at the back, standing alone, has lost its support. Because of the other tooth's absence, the whole dynamic of the lineup has changed."

I was glad when he stopped talking and began working so I could close my eyes and think. About Nate.

When a husband dies, a wife remains standing under the new burden of widowhood, much like my unconnected tooth continued standing alone. She muscles through the necessary adjustments, as my cheek tried to do, but is well aware her marriage dynamic has dramatically changed. The initial pain of missing her man begins to escalate, eventually becoming an ache in her soul.

My dentist put a little cement on the bridge and restored my tooth lineup, and although my jaw still hurt, he promised time would make it feel better. He could do nothing, however, to heal my heart.

Thankfully, God can. According to Scripture, "The Lord is close to the brokenhearted and saves those who are crushed in spirit" (Psalm 34:18). He's in the process of establishing a new dynamic for me, although it's more complicated than re-cementing a bridge. But I know somehow God will close the gap, and with time, I'll feel better.

For now, though, the dentist told me there *is* something I can do. "Lay off the bubble gum for a while."

> *[The Lord] restores my soul.*
> Psalm 23:3 (NKJV)

Lord, as you align my life in a new way, please refresh my soul. Amen.

28

Initiating Traditions

Every family has its traditions, and most families work hard to create happy memories through them. Children find security in the routine of "we've always done that . . . always visited them . . . always gone there."

Just as children love to read and reread the same storybook, they love repeating times of family togetherness. Our kids used to ask, "Are we going on that same vacation again this year?" Beneath their question they were asking, "Are we the same family we were last year? Does everybody still love everybody else?" Establishing and repeating traditions can be a first-rate family stabilizer.

Nate was the creative force behind most of our traditions, everything from vacation destinations to holiday menus to the mini-traditions of Saturday morning donuts, Friday night pizza, and Sunday noon brunches. Regular customs like these served as anchors for our family, but when death removed their initiator, the traditions lost their luster.

Although our family trudged through that first year without Nate by hanging on to our rituals, our hope of holding onto him by doing so didn't work. His absence was painful, and we concluded if we couldn't have him, we didn't want his traditions either. As for establishing new ones without him, it was a no-go.

While thinking about all this, we discovered something interesting. God has family traditions, too, and has invited us to enjoy the stability they offer. Scripture reading, prayer, and church attendance allow us to receive His gifts of understanding and insight. And there's more: baptism, communion, and others. As we participate in these traditions, we receive the answer to our underlying question of "Do you still love us, Lord?" Through these activities He says yes!

Paul wrote, "Follow my example, as I follow the example of Christ. I praise you for . . . holding to the traditions just as I passed them on to you" (1 Corinthians 11:1–2). Our family traditions were initiated by Nate; God's traditions find headship in Christ.

Although Nate is no longer part of our earthly family, it's uplifting to know that in his heavenly home he's still participating in many of the same traditions we enjoy: talking to Jesus, worshipping God, and fellowshipping with other believers. These things we still do "together."

The second year after Nate died, we cautiously started new family traditions and resumed a few old ones. Slowly these took hold, bringing our altered family a measure of stability, even without Nate. As for God's traditions, they'll never need revamping, because His family will never be in danger of losing its Leader.

> *Every year Jesus' parents went to Jerusalem*
> *for the Festival of the Passover.*
> Luke 2:41

Lord, thank you for the traditions you've established that anchor me to you when I feel lost. Amen.

29

Diagnosis: Hopeless

Life has a long list of things we take for granted until they disappear. Then we regret not appreciating what we had when we had it. Good health is on that list. Nate's health lasted sixty years before the red flags began to wave: colon polyps, skewed prostate numbers, and severe back pain. He visited specialists recommended by friends and faithfully followed instructions, after which the first two problems disappeared. He was in the process of tackling the third when cancer arrived, and no one was able to remedy that.

Nate knew how fortunate he'd been to have six decades of hale-and-hearty. When it ended, he knew he'd be crushed physically but was determined not to let cancer crush him emotionally. He understood nothing could have prevented his cancer so he didn't spend one minute bemoaning his assignment. Instead he adopted a mind-set of stoic acceptance. As a result, when his physical vigor diminished, his emotions remained steady.

Lately I've wondered about my own health. Watching my husband go through his calamity taught me a great deal about how to weather my own storm, whenever it comes.

At some point good health will end for me. Short of a sudden accident, I'll sit in a doctor's office and receive bad news just as Nate did. It's logical and inevitable. When that moment comes, whether later or sooner, I hope God taps me on the shoulder with a reminder: accept the news as Nate did.

Hearing of a serious health crisis will make that difficult, but I hope when my bad news comes, I'll turn toward God within seconds, before anguish can get its evil grip on me. As the Great Physician, God will still be making house calls and will arrive armed with a doctor's bag packed with remedies for every emotional ill. Though I'll be tempted to sink toward gloom, fear, and hopelessness, God is able to doctor these disturbing feelings and repair hurting emotions every time.

Psalm 30:2 says, "Lord my God, I called to you for help, and you healed me." This doesn't necessarily mean physical healing. Not one of us understands why He doesn't perform miraculous healings in every case, but we shouldn't waste time wondering. Instead we should focus on what He *does* do as He faithfully heals us of despair. He's a loving fixer who readily awaits our calls.

Eventually God will use the power behind His promises to correct every physical problem we have, but we won't experience it until our diagnosis seems completely hopeless. When it's my turn to walk through terminal illness, I want to remember that when death gets ready to roar in triumph, exactly then I'll be gloriously healed!

He sent out his word and healed them;
he rescued them from the grave.
Psalm 107:20

Lord, give me enthusiastic appreciation for each day I'm in good health, and prepare me thoroughly for any crisis that's ahead. Amen.

30

A New Me

Marriage is described in the Bible as two becoming one (see Genesis 2:24). A simple visual might be a husband and wife sharing one umbrella, huddled close, clutching the handle together. The two are inside the one.

Widowhood is a loss of that oneness, which necessitates standing alone beneath the umbrella. This unplanned independence has a familiar feel to it, since "solo" was the starting point for all of us. But standing alone in widowhood doesn't feel right. We can't hold our umbrella as straight as it used to be. It flops from side to side, and after managing it alone for a while, we become tired.

Those of us who were married for decades find ourselves wondering what's going to happen next. Some hurry into a second marriage, feeling lonely and uncomfortable with the mantle of singleness. Others try to turn back the clock hoping to remake youth's decisions: a new job, a new hairdo, a new wardrobe.

A few risk their savings on precarious ventures in a quest for the income husbands once provided. A small number hurt so badly that they burrow into widowhood as a permanent identity.

When I became a widow, wise advisers told me not to make any changes for a year. "Don't move back to Chicago. Don't give away Nate's clothes. Don't join anything. Don't quit anything. Don't even rearrange your furniture."

In this recommended holding pattern of refusing to change, we widows find ourselves yearning for a revised life purpose. Eventually the "don'ts" must morph into "dos." Although earthly life ended for our men, it didn't end for us. None of us should be fooled into thinking we can stay in a partnership that is no more.

God has a positive purpose for our remaining years, something separate from our marriages and our men. Half-plus-half made a marriage whole. Now we're half-minus-half, and it's difficult not to think of ourselves as incomplete. All of us want to be whole.

The remedy is to accept God's offer to fill us completely, making us whole in Him. Romans 15:13 says, "May the God of hope fill you with all joy and peace as you trust in him, so that you may overflow with hope by the power of the Holy Spirit." He wants to grow us into a brand new whole without our husbands, one that is filled with joy and peace, and brimming with hope.

Embracing a fresh start is scary, because we love the familiar. But as we tentatively step with Him into the worrisome unknown, we'll eventually realize we don't even need our umbrellas anymore, because the sun has come out and is shining brighter than ever.

> *"From now on I will tell you of new things . . .*
> *They are created now, and not long ago;*
> *you have not heard of them before today."*
> Isaiah 48:6–7

Lord, now that my husband is gone, I look to you for the details of my new beginning. Amen.

Part 4

Learning to Live
without Him

31

Feeling Numb

In the days following Nate's funeral, I wondered how long it would be before we adjusted to life without him. Since he died in November, I figured by spring we'd all feel much better. But when spring came, life seemed sadder than ever, and I couldn't think or talk about anyone but him. I related to Job's misery when he said, "If I speak, my pain is not relieved; and if I refrain, it does not go away" (16:6). My children, too, talked of missing their father more than ever.

Widow friends warned me about this stage.

After terminal illness terminates, loved ones are left feeling cold and lifeless, even numb. Just like a dentist numbs our jaw to mask intolerable physical pain, I believe God numbs our thinking, at least in the beginning, to mask intolerable emotional pain. It's as if He freezes the feelings-center of the brain so we can continue to function.

Some months later, though, when we're ready, He allows a gradual wake-up, just as a jaw regains feeling when Novocain wears away. And that's what my family was experiencing in the spring as our feelings returned. The new normal without Nate became a deep, gnawing ache.

Sometimes, when in the dentist's chair, I'll get a zap of pain while he's drilling and I'll say, "Ow!" He'll take his instruments from my mouth and administer a bit more Novocain. Then he'll wait to be sure I can't feel anything before proceeding. God operated the same way during our numb months, letting us think and talk about how sad we were without Nate but not letting us feel the permanent "ouch" of reality.

Eventually it was time to come out of our numbness, and God withdrew it gently, knowing a new kind of pain would begin. But He let us experience the hurt of our new reality only as we could tolerate it. One precious widow friend told me she pleaded with God to bring back her numbness.

But of course none of us wants to stay numb forever.

After the dentist makes a jaw numb, it's no fun to eat, talk, or even smile until the Novocain wears off. Emotional numbness is much like that. Life can't be really good again if we can't feel it. The only thing to do is come out of the numbness and trust God to manage our pain tolerance while we do. He's available to assist as needed, and best of all, He knows exactly when to stop the Novocain, and when to wait.

> *The Lord longs to be gracious to you;*
> *therefore he will rise up to show you compassion.*
> Isaiah 30:18

Lord, I long to move away from numbness but need you to monitor my pain. Please show me how to cope. Amen.

32

Missing Kissing

One of the pleasures of being married is the unlimited kisses that come along with it. As a widow, I really miss Nate's kisses.

Although most widows are mum about the loss of physical intimacy after a husband dies, all of us feel the loss. For me, the loneliest time of every day is crawling into bed without him, missing the absence of the warm togetherness we shared there. The God-ordained idea of "two becoming one" is deeply missed, including the kisses and everything that goes along with them.

It's comforting to realize there are other kinds of kisses besides those between husbands and wives. In Scripture we see believers greeting each other with kisses and kings kissing their subjects; there are hello-kisses and good-bye-kisses, and kisses between parents and children.

Scripture uses the imagery of kisses in some colorful ways. One example occurs in Psalm 85 where we're told of believers who've gone astray but then have turned back and are ready to submit to the Lord again. The psalmist vividly describes God's character in relation to these people who are eager to glean the benefits of a restored relationship: "Love and faithfulness meet together; righteousness and peace kiss each other . . . The Lord will indeed give what is good" (verses 10–12).

Why did God use the word *kiss* here? Maybe it's because kisses bring two people together in a unique way. Contact is close, intimate, personal. A kiss is full of poignant meaning, arising from affection and love. Although we can't physically kiss the Lord, we can regain some of what we miss about our husbands when we draw close to Him in intimate, personal communication. Psalm 85 mentions nearly a dozen goodies God wants to share with us when we come, like restoration, forgiveness, love, salvation, peace, faithfulness, and righteousness.

Another interesting kiss-reference in the Bible is found in Proverbs: "An honest answer is like a kiss on the lips" (24:26). This probably applies to our being honest with Him, too. As we truthfully pour out our sorrows, it just might feel as good as a kiss. We can even envision ourselves face-to-face with Him, which is exactly what Psalm 27:8 invites us to do.

God knows some of us learn best through pictures, which may be why He uses the imagery of kisses to explain how tenderly He wants to help us. We widows may have lost touch with husbandly kisses, but we can still benefit from seeking His face. When we do, we'll learn what it feels like to received the scriptural kisses He intends for us to have.

Greet one another with a kiss of love.
Peace to all of you who are in Christ.
1 Peter 5:14

Lord, when I'm missing the physical intimacy I used to enjoy with my husband, please come as close as a kiss on the lips, breathing your love into my soul. Amen.

33

Discombobulated

When the kitchen sink clogs, I can figure it out. When a drawer sticks or the upholstery rips, I know what to do. When fuses blow again and again, I don't have a clue. My electric water heater with its own little fuse box and an on-off lever looks straightforward, but when there should be hot water in the tank, there isn't.

But only sometimes.

I have resorted to flipping the lever "on" to heat up a tank of water (while standing back to avoid sparks), and then flipping it to "off" afterward. During the night I worry the house will burn down and wonder how likely that is. The whole thing is a fresh opportunity to miss Nate. He wasn't an electrician, but at least we could have discussed a next step.

We new widows feel especially vulnerable to minor mishaps like blown fuses, and any small blip in circumstances can quickly grow into a crisis, at least as we view it. Of course we can use a phone as well as the next person, but we often have trouble making the tiny decisions necessary to get that far. "Who do I call? What if I get swindled? Can I trust a stranger coming into my home? Will the repair be expensive? Will the whole electrical system have to be replaced?" A succession of paralyzing questions stresses us.

Scripture reinforces the idea that God does everything in an orderly way. The word "careful" appears many times in the biblical descriptions of everything from creation to the end times. It's all step-by-step. As to my dilemma with the hot water heater, Deuteronomy 5:32 tells me to "be careful to do what the Lord your God has commanded you; do not turn aside to the right or to the left." That would have given me the solution to my problem, if only God had commanded me what to do! As I stood paralyzed by indecision, my mind was hopping left, then right, then left, unable to find that center-lane sweet spot of step-by-step.

The best-meaning widow becomes incapacitated with too many options, coupled with the ever-present angst of ongoing grief. What often seems best is to do nothing at all. In the months since Nate died, I've found myself locked in a swirl of indecision again and again, to the point of wondering if I should walk upstairs to get my shoes or downstairs to start the laundry. Either would be fine, and both have to be done, but there I've stood in the living room, unable to move.

Life becomes discombobulated when a woman loses her mate to death. Nate was good at making decisions and acted without hesitation, either by making a call or promising to have a solution by the next day. But because he's gone, the other half of the conversation is missing, throwing me into a tailspin of uncertainty.

I have high hopes my decision-confusion will eventually lift. Long-term widows tell me it will. In the meantime, I'm asking God what to do about my hot water heater, and because His response to my needs is never discombobulated, I'm certain He'll point me to a step-by-step solution. My confidence rests in Him.

> *Do not throw away your confidence; it will be*
> *richly rewarded. You need to persevere.*
> Hebrews 10:35–36

Lord, when I don't know what to do next, please order my thoughts so I can make the decisions I need to make. Amen.

34

Counting the Days

How do you celebrate a wedding anniversary with only half of a couple? Nate and I were married on Thanksgiving weekend in 1969. The year he died we would have been married forty years but fell short by twenty-six days.

We met on a blind date back in 1966. A girlfriend had promised to set me up with a good-looking college senior she knew and called late one night after I'd stuffed most of my wardrobe into the washer and was sitting in my flannels, reading in bed. "We ran into him at the ice cream parlor," she said, "and he wants to meet you. Now!"

I complained about her poor timing but dug out my navy "dress coat" and put it over my underwear. As I met the man of my dreams, his first words were, "May I take your coat?" He asked three times during the evening, but I resisted as we ate our chocolate sundaes.

My friend later chided me for being unfriendly. "You wouldn't even let him take your coat!"

"Actually," I said while unbuttoning, "here's why." She looked at my underwear and burst out laughing.

Forty years and seven children later, Nate knew the truth about our blind date. He always got nervous when he asked, "May I take your coat?"

That funny beginning set the tone for our marriage. Even on serious days, there was always something to smile about. On the morning of my first anniversary without him, the first thing I saw was a note slipped under my bedroom door. My daughter Louisa had penned encouragement around a picture of the two of us: "I want to restate what you always encouraged me with: 'The Lord heals the broken-hearted and binds up their wounds' (Psalm 147:3). Like you said, Mom, 'It's a promise!' I miss Papa like crazy, too."

Smiling through tears, I felt a twinge of healing.

Just to be safe, though, I tucked several tissues between the pages of my Bible for tears during church and got ready for another difficult "first" without Nate. To my surprise I never needed the tissues. Instead I sat in the service thinking of the blessings in our years together. Though we had only six weeks of warning before our earthly partnership ended, it would be tragic to dwell on the sadness of those 42 days rather than the fullness of the other 14,584.

Nate's desire was to celebrate our fortieth anniversary together, and if he'd had a choice, he would have been there with flowers, a present, and maybe a weekend getaway. But in his absence, God gave me a wonderful gift, a promise He made during the Scripture reading at church: "I, the Lord, have called you in righteousness; I will take hold of your hand. I will keep you" (Isaiah 42:6).

> *This is what the Lord says—". . . Do not fear, for I have redeemed you; I have summoned you by name; you are mine."*
> Isaiah 43:1

Lord, when I'm dwelling on my losses, bring me back to counting blessings. Amen.

35

Language Barrier

Before I became a widow, I heard horror stories from friends about the nightmare of paperwork following a spouse's death. Some wives are naturally skilled to understand taxes, insurance policies, balance sheets, and investments.

Not me.

I remember the discouraging day a few weeks after Nate died when I had four online, data-related jobs to accomplish in partnership with the World Wide Web. The thought paralyzed me, because I knew I would fail again and again. So I had put it off as long as I could.

When I finally went online, my first inclination was to search for 800 numbers so I could get off-line. When I was lucky enough to reach another human on the phone, every person said the same thing: "Why don't you just do it online? It's easy!"

My son Nelson told me that the trick to communicating with a computer is to learn how to give commands it understands. "Try to learn its language," he said. Once I saw it that way, I began to make progress by learning computer vocabulary.

That same principle holds true in my relationship with God. When I talk to Him, I need to speak appropriately and then listen well. Sometimes He calls to me and I might say, "I don't need you right now." That response doesn't use the right vocabulary and damages our relationship. If He says, "I've got good plans for you," I might say, "But I like my own plans." Bad language again. It's like right-clicking when a left is needed.

In John 8 Jesus was teaching simply and clearly, but His listeners still misunderstood Him. He asked them a question, and then answered it himself: "Why is my language not clear to you? Because you are unable to hear what I say" (verse 43). The conversation wasn't going well because those listening weren't understanding the message behind His words.

As I communicate with God, it's paramount I listen with an open mind and speak to Him from a submissive heart. Why? Going back to the scriptural story, Jesus eventually made a potent point: "Whoever belongs to God hears what God says" (verse 47).

I'm sure I belong to Him, so I know I'm capable of hearing what He says. And I want to communicate back appropriately. The more I practice this, the better my spiritual language becomes.

As we widows wade through paperwork and stumble along on our computers, eventually we'll learn how to "speak" our requests properly through the keyboard, and the desired cyber-pages will open. Once we learn how to communicate well with God, He'll open a channel of widow-understanding that might even let us converse fluently with a computer.

May these words of my mouth and this meditation of my heart
be pleasing in your sight, Lord, my Rock and my Redeemer.
Psalm 19:14

Lord, although my understanding of record-keeping may be limited, please cause my understanding of you to always be increasing. Amen.

36

Afraid of the Dark

When Jack and I take our late-night walks through the neighborhood each evening, the tree-shaded streets are inky black. I always grab a flashlight, because without it, both of us would walk into parked cars and yard fences trying to find our way.

Most of my flashlights are the dollar store variety. Their circle of light is small and often inadequate, although a little light is better than none. Then there is my heavy flashlight that has a powerful halogen bulb. When I carry that one, I feel guilty for producing a beam of light that spills into the privacy of people's living rooms. It's a floodlight in a tube.

Recently when Jack and I were out walking, my cheap flashlight flickered with weak batteries, casting only a faint glow in front of us. My first choice would have been to see all the way down the road, but my light would only shine as far as the next spot my foot would land and no farther. Although it was frustrating, at least it kept us on the right path.

Scripture gives us a word picture of this exact situation. *"Your Word is a lamp* for my feet, and a light on my path" (Psalm 119:105, italics added). Now that I'm walking a widow's path, I crave a peek down the road into my future, preferring a floodlight to a flashlight or a lamp. Not being able to see where I'm headed leads to worry and fear.

God is the only one who can see all the way down the road. Because of that, it seems sensible to leave the darkness and uncertainty of what's ahead up to Him. He'll highlight what I need to know, when

I need to know it. Meanwhile, He hands me the lamp of His Word and says, "One step is enough for now. Walk into that small circle of light right in front of you, and let me take care of what's ahead in the dark."

On our walk with the faulty flashlight, Jack offered the perfect example of why we ought to take God's advice on this. He stepped in front of my flashlight's beam, which suddenly cast his own black shadow directly in front of him. He startled, jumped to the side, and searched for the dark villain he'd just encountered, which of course had disappeared. The walk went better when he stayed behind the light and followed where it led.

That's good advice for me, too.

Even the darkness will not be dark to you; the night will shine like the day, for darkness is as light to you.
Psalm 139:12

Lord, please help me find time to look at the lamp of your Word. Teach me to be content with enough light for only the next step, surrendering the darkness to you. Amen.

37

Clothes Don't Make the Man

All of us know we're supposed to hold our possessions lightly, but it doesn't come naturally to us. The Bible says, "Every good and perfect gift is from above, coming down from the Father of the heavenly lights" (James 1:17). Our "stuff" has come to us, in one way or another, from God. After Nate died, his belongings seemed to become extra "good and perfect." I did not want to give them away.

My first reaction was to leave everything as it was: the pens atop his dresser, his shoes lined up in a row, his suits on the closet bar. Bundling it up for charity was too big a task, and so everything remained as he left it.

When I finally decided it was time to deal with at least part of Nate's wardrobe, eighteen months had gone by. His business shirts had been hanging in dry cleaner plastic ready to go to work all those months, despite Nate's work having been finished. How foolish not to let other workers wear them.

Much of adjusting to widowhood is emotional and must first be done in our heads. It's really not about the shirts but about missing the guy who was inside them. Adaline Bjorkman, in her book *While It Was Still Dark*, said it well: "Your clothes hanging lifeless in the closet bear testimony to the precious you they clothed." Reminding myself that Nate isn't ever going to wear those shirts again helped me let them go. I don't want to cling to a fantasy.

Jesus had something to say about clothes: "Do not worry about . . . your body, what you will wear. Is not . . . the body more than clothes?"

(Matthew 6:25). Clothes are nothing without a person inside of them, and Nate's shirts should mean little to me without him wearing them.

It helped to think of Nate's shirts as being recycled rather than disposed of. They would be buttoned around another man somewhere who would benefit from having them. Looking at the clothes in that way made it seem honorable and wise to donate them to charity.

A day will come for each of us when we won't need what's hanging in our closets. On that day, whether we slip out of this life through illness or accident, closet contents won't matter at all. It brings perspective to the clothing issue today if we picture others pawing through and disposing of our things tomorrow, after we've gone to heaven.

Nate is currently wearing an outfit from a supernatural wardrobe that would put his earthly clothes to shame. Holding on to shirts that don't measure up to that standard just seems silly.

> *There before me was a great multitude that no one*
> *could count . . . standing before the throne and before*
> *the Lamb. They were wearing white robes . . .*
> Revelation 7:9

Lord, enable me to pass along my husband's possessions to those who really need them. Amen.

38

Fantasyland

All of us are good at enhancing the truth, especially widows. We watch other couples and assume they live in perfect harmony; that makes us agonize over no longer being married. We imagine everyone else surrounded by groups of loved ones; that makes us anxious about living alone. We envision flawless fathering in other families; that makes us stress over our children, who miss their dad.

Mental pictures of perfection in others' lives are pure fantasy, and if we aren't careful, we can be swamped by these lies. Holidays, especially, are prime for letting our imaginations run wild. We cry on Valentine's Day, thinking we're the only ones not wrapped in another's arms. On Mother's Day we feel sorry for ourselves because everyone but us seems to have a parenting partner. At Christmas we study greeting cards and are saddened when our family isn't picture-perfect. And on New Year's Eve, while watching the whole world embrace a new year, we wonder how we'll even live through it.

It's important to remember that what appears idyllic probably isn't, and being jealous of a fairy tale is silly. We hope our lives will match the delectable pictures that have invaded our minds, but most things aren't as they seem, and spending time wishing for non-reality is foolishness. Believing that everyone has a lover on Valentine's Day or that Christmas card fantasies are reality should be labeled "worldly wisdom," and we know what God thinks of that.

The Bible says, "The wisdom of this world is foolishness in God's sight" (1 Corinthians 3:19). This hints that the best way to find widow-wisdom on how to handle holidays is to ask God. After all, His advice is flawless. In addition, every holiday finds its origin in Him. For example, Valentine's Day is about love, and Scripture tells us God *is* love (1 John 4:8). Mother's Day is about children, and Psalms says children are a gift from God (Psalm 127:3–5). Christmas is about the birth of God's Son (Luke 1:31–33). And a New Year's celebration is about new beginnings, each one a gift from God (Lamentations 3:22–23).

Holidays were never about us or our husbands. They've always been about Him.

When our celebrations don't resemble the fantasies we see in greeting card aisles, we should shake off those lies and run to God, knowing He's ready to bring something new into our old holiday traditions. As each celebration approaches, we'll find satisfaction in it if we first shift our focus from the husbands who are missing, to the One who is still with us.

Jesus is a pro at togetherness. After all, His first name is Immanuel, and it means, "God with us."

> *The virgin will conceive and give birth to a son,*
> *and they will call him Immanuel (which means "God with us").*
> Matthew 1:23

Lord, pull me from every holiday fantasy and rivet my attention on you instead. Amen.

39

I Just Forgot

Losing half of a marriage couple changes more than half of a woman's life. She has to think differently in every category, except maybe hair and makeup.

At Nate's funeral, my cousin Cal gently reminded me that the areas of our marriage that Nate used to handle would now have to be handled by me. For instance, Nate always made the coffee, put salt in the water softener, arranged the vacations, and managed insurance policies. Cal said, "If you can't do what Nate used to do, ask for help. Just be sure those things aren't left undone."

My problem comes in noticing what needs doing. While Cal was in town, the family left the house for several hours and returned to find seven candles still burning on the mantle. Nate would never have stepped out the door without blowing them out, but I hadn't noticed. It made me wonder what else was being left undone because of his absence.

Every married couple works out who does what in the relationship. Now after decades of competently handling the tasks we always did, we widows find ourselves needing to handle his jobs, too. Suddenly we are inefficient and incompetent in these new areas. We need the assistance of others, and we also need God's guidance to find trustworthy aides to fill the void our husbands left behind.

I love Psalm 10:14: "You, God, see the trouble of the afflicted; you consider their grief and take it in hand." The leadership our husbands used to provide is now His responsibility. He'll "take it in hand." The picture is of Him stepping in to dismantle our troubles, and when we forget to complete a new responsibility, He'll help us with damage control.

The day my cousin visited he gently said, "I'll bet Nate made sure the house was locked up each night. Are you doing that?"

It was no surprise I wasn't. Actually, the house hadn't been locked for weeks. I just kept forgetting to do it. These seemingly endless surprises kept me off-balance, but surprises are the name of the game for widows. Piled on top of one another, they make for a day of defeat unless we remember one important thing: to let God lead. With Him before us (see Deuteronomy 31:8), it's possible to get to the end of each day with hope that tomorrow we just might not forget what needs to be done.

> *Wisdom will enter your heart, and knowledge will be*
> *pleasant to your soul. Discretion will protect you,*
> *and understanding will guard you.*
> Proverbs 2:10–11

Lord, when I feel like I can't handle my new assignment as a widow, please grant me your wisdom, knowledge, and understanding. And prompt me to remember! Amen.

40

A Crystallized Future

Most people want to know what's ahead. Some pay fortune-tellers to try to find out, or read palms, tea leaves, or crystal balls. But is it an advantage to know?

As Nate and I moved from Illinois to Michigan in the month of June, we had no idea a terminal cancer diagnosis was coming in September. In September we didn't know he'd die in November. Would we have done things differently, had we known? Would we have rushed off to complete a bucket list? Or invited a string of visitors? Or eaten more chocolate? Fixed more lobster? Toured Europe? Probably not.

Even during Nate's forty-two days of diagnosed cancer, it was beneficial to be unaware of how little time we had left or exactly what those six weeks would look like. What if Van's Medical Supply had arrived with all twenty-one pieces of hospital equipment at once? We would have gasped in disbelief. Taking health steps downward one at a time was better than being shoved down the whole staircase.

Or what if the hospice nurse had said, "By the end of this, you'll be keeping track of thirty-eight different medicines, each with different instructions"?

I'd have said, "Not a chance." But as the prescriptions increased, my ability to manage them did, too. And that was the beauty of not knowing. God was always one step ahead, equipping us as necessary.

So, what about life as a widow? Is it beneficial to know how that's going to go? Since I don't, I have nothing specific to fret about. Instead I look back at God's detailed handling of everything before Nate's diagnosis and during the cancer, and I see He skillfully sorted through multitudes of unknowns with expertise and timeliness.

He delivered what I needed, just before I needed it. At one point I pictured Him walking ahead of me with a big machete, slashing at obstacles on my path. When I couldn't see a way through, He created one. So I know that I'll be able to keep moving forward as a widow no matter what the future brings, because God has already proven himself capable.

Psalm 139:5 says, "You hem me in behind and before, and you lay your hand upon me." That's a secure place to be, in front of, behind, and underneath the Lord's care. It's natural to crave knowledge of the future, but it is best to simply place our trust in the One who already sees our tomorrows.

And He doesn't even need a crystal ball.

As the mountains surround Jerusalem,
so the Lord surrounds his people both now and forevermore.
Psalm 125:2

Lord, give me the courage to fully trust that you'll prepare me for every detail of my uncertain future. Nothing is uncertain to you. Amen.

Part 5

Finding New Peace

41

It's Up to You

Nate was raised in a town of thirty thousand, but his first job as an attorney was in a city of three million. We'd been married two and a half years when we left law school for Chicago's Loop, and I was thrilled to be "back home." Nate loved the city and adjusted quickly to its fast pace and new logistics.

After thirty-eight jam-packed years in Chicago, it was time to simplify and begin slowing down. Nate wasn't feeling well, and his high-stress job was taking a toll. Consequently, we sold our suburban home and moved to a much smaller cottage on the other side of Lake Michigan. We were nervous about how life would be in a tiny town far from all things familiar—our church, neighborhood, family, and friends—but viewed it as a sixty-something adventure.

Although our Illinois calendar had been over-inked with commitments, our Michigan calendar was virtually empty, and life became more manageable and delightfully peaceful. That summer I wrote in my journal, "Here I am, ready for a new phase of life."

I had no clue my "new phase" would be nursing a terminally ill husband, followed by getting used to life without him. At the end of that same entry I wrote an optimistic prayer: "I wait at your feet, Lord, for instructions, opportunities, your revealing of the path I'm to walk. Whatever it is, it's up to you."

Nate's cancer crisis arrived shortly after that, and even while it was ongoing, I couldn't deny God had answered my prayer. I'd told Him I was ready for "a new phase," and He'd given it to me.

The problem was, I disliked His choice.

That's the thing about following God's lead. He may choose something distasteful to us, and it can be especially difficult to follow as a result. But if we ask Him to lead and He does, we can either fight against the circumstances He brings or agree that His plans are best. We can obey or go our own way.

However, it's helpful to remember that the very best thinking we can do is never as good (or complete or farsighted) as His. Jeremiah 29:11 starts with a potent statement by God: "I know the plans I have for you." He *knows*. He's sure. He's confident they're best, but He never forces us to cooperate. He leaves it up to us to sign on . . . or not.

After Nate died and I became a widow, I prayed my prayer again. "Now what, Lord? What instructions, opportunities?" I knew God had already gone ahead of me and thought through my alternatives before giving me this challenging new phase. So I'm cooperating with Him and know, without doubt, life will get better as I follow His lead.

> *When you received the word of God . . . you accepted it*
> *not as a human word, but as it actually is, the word of God,*
> *which is indeed at work in you who believe.*
> 1 Thessalonians 2:13

Lord, give me the determination and confidence to follow your lead, even when the going gets rough. Amen.

42

A Blizzard of Emotions

Nate and I always loved summer best. Our birthdays were both in August, which established summertime as party time, often at a beach. Our own children added two more summer birthdays, and even without the excuse of a party, there was no destination more fun than a big lake.

Even so, I'd never dispute the loveliness of spring or majesty of autumn. But a month after Nate died, I found myself in nature's fourth season, bleak winter. Michigan snowstorms clawed at my windows, and the car was buried in snow. My driveway needed frequent shoveling, while tall trees bent ominously, nearly giving in to nature's forceful winds. In addition to all this, my heart and emotions were experiencing a winter of their own.

I've always disliked winter's cold, partly because I hate to shiver but mostly because it's the opposite of summer's warm invitation to come out and play. But during my first winter without a husband, God proved that every season has its glories. One day when Jack needed a walk, I bundled up during a storm and we struck out for nearby Lake Michigan. Despite tasting sand mixed with flying snow, I had to admit the dunes looked like a giant bowl of fudge ripple ice cream. Suddenly I forgot all about summertime as I reveled in the splendor of a beach blizzard.

Every season has its own appeal, and that's true of life's seasons too. When Nate died, the process of letting him go felt much like an icy winter day. As we held onto him throughout his transition from this world to the next, his body quickly became cold and lifeless. But God reminded us right then that the best summer of his life had just begun in a place where death's coldness is nonexistent. Nate had stepped into the warmth of paradise.

Scripture tells me, "[The Lord] has done everything well" (Mark 7:37), and that includes allowing winter, both in the outdoors and in our emotions. A fresh crop of troubles will most assuredly come, but God promises to be "an ever-present help in trouble" (Psalm 46:1). I'm thankful for the sixty-five beachside summers I've experienced, as well as my warm emotional summers. But I'm also grateful for the other seasons, and by faith that includes winter, too.

Contrary to nature's winters, which don't produce crops at all, our emotional winters often yield the most abundant harvests of our lives.

As long as the earth remains, there will be planting and harvest,
cold and heat, summer and winter, day and night.
Genesis 8:22 (NLT)

Lord, when I'm feeling cold and storm-battered, draw me close to your warmth. Amen.

43

An Empty Calendar

Most of us buy a new calendar or planner in late autumn for the upcoming year. Time moves relentlessly, sweeping us into new weeks, months, and years, and life demands we plan ahead. Sometimes, however, it's valuable to look back.

Two weeks after Nate's November death, I came home with a new wall calendar. As I put the old and new side by side on the dining room table to transfer birthdays, the new calendar could have said to the old one, "You've got the answers now, but I'm still a big question mark."

I turned to the pages with their markings of Nate's descent from good health. The daily squares were crowded with doctor appointments, radiation treatments, hospice visits, scans, equipment deliveries, and names of guests. Between those lines in green marker was written: first fall, restlessness, weak legs, family photo, won't eat, friends say good-bye, can't drink. At the start of that year, none of us could have imagined these shocking words on the calendar squares.

Studying my new, unmarked calendar, I worried about what might end up written on it. How do we live in hope and with optimism when we know we'll meet with negative surprises in coming days? How do we focus on life when each day we step closer to death?

Nate used to tap the glass on his watch with his index finger and say, "Nobody beats this guy." We rush through life, well aware we can't stop time. Since we're given twenty-four hours every day, we do our best to cram in all we can, to write as much on each calendar square as will fit. But it's a good idea to keep sight of the truth that each of us will one day come to a square with our end-date on it, as Nate did. On November 3, my old calendar says, "Nate went to heaven, 7:35 p.m." No more squares for him.

If we stay mindful that each of us has a final day, we'll carefully consider what gets written on our calendars. Is busy always better? Should Wite-Out be kept handy? Are blank days cause for panic?

The healthiest way to approach a new calendar is to remind ourselves we know very little about the upcoming year. Thankfully, though, God looks at our blank calendars like we look at the year just past—He already sees what's written in each square. We can turn over our clean calendars to Him before our pens touch the paper, and when we do, apprehension over "calendar question marks" will vanish.

A thousand years in your sight are like a day that has just
gone by . . . Satisfy us in the morning with your unfailing love,
that we may sing for joy and be glad all our days.
Psalm 90:4, 14

Lord, please take charge of my calendar. I release my anxieties over my unknown future and thank you for going into it with me. Amen.

44

Family Changes

Before pancreatic cancer invaded our family, we received news of a third grandbaby on the way. Daughter Linnea and her husband, Adam, would be adding a new family member the following February, and we happily spread the good word. Not long after that, additional delightful news came, this time from our son Hans and his wife, Katy. They, too, would be increasing our clan with a baby due in April.

Then the awful news of terminal disease yanked our attention away, and medical woes swept us into hospital halls and testing rooms. But one fine day, as Linnea, Nate, and I were driving home from Nate's ninth radiation treatment, my cell phone rang. It was Hans from England, with Katy on the extension.

"How did the ultrasound go today?" I asked.

"OK, but they did find a little something," he said. "A second baby's in there!"

The news left us nearly speechless, but we did manage to fill the car with squeals of delight and joyful congratulations.

I looked over at Nate, who was tipped all the way back in his passenger seat, eyes closed, face pinched in pain. "Hans and Katy are having *twins*!" I said.

Although he managed a smile and gently clapped his hands, he was too weary for anything more. I pushed away the thought that he might not live to meet his three new little relatives.

Nate died months before the births and is not in the hundreds of photos we've taken since then. Two of these little ones are boys, both named after him.

After Nate died, our hospice friends warned us that the birth of each new baby would prompt both rejoicing and grieving. They wanted us to be aware that as we met and got to know Micah Nathan, Thomas Nathan, and Evelyn Sarah, we'd have some sorrowful moments because of Nate's absence. These are relationships he will never know and vice versa.

The death of a loved one ruins much about life, including relationships for the unborn. God has plans to correct that predicament and will one day rid the world of death. In the meantime, He tells us what we're to do. He says, "I have set before you life and death, blessings and curses. Now choose life" (Deuteronomy 30:19).

We can curse our losses, focusing on death's gains. Or we can highlight life, rejoicing in God's plan for us to share eternal joy. In this world we'll always be surrounded by a mix of curses and blessings, but as God says, we can make it our business to always choose life.

Love the Lord your God,
listen to his voice, and hold fast to him.
Deuteronomy 30:20

Lord, show me how to appreciate the relationships I have today, being conscious of the fragile nature of life on earth. Amen.

45

Hidden Biographies

Most TV game shows are a study in psychology. I recall one program that was easy to play but sometimes revealed embarrassing secrets. The host walked through the audience waving a hundred dollar bill, looking for a willing participant.

Once he chose a contestant he might say, "Do you have a wooden match in your purse?" (Or a baby picture or a deck of cards.) If she produced the item he asked for, he'd hand her the one-hundred dollar bill. Occasionally a woman would empty her whole purse, flinging lipstick and keys in the laps of those nearby, frantic to find the winning item.

People say a woman's biography can be written by the contents of her purse: money, makeup, pens, keys, glasses, receipts, gum, and the like. Each item has been carefully chosen to be carried in her purse, and therein lies the biography.

Several months after Nate died, I needed some Post-it notes and opened his dresser drawer to get them. Although I'd given away many of his things, the three top drawers in his highboy were still as he'd left them. Just like a woman's purse, they said a great deal about who he was: a lint roller, a knife for filleting fish (in a leather case), business cards (his own and others), shirt collar stays, current contact information for our children, his watch (still ticking), a commuter train schedule, a tiny eyeglass fix-it kit, a Nixon tie clip, pens, check blanks, and other practical items.

As I fingered each thing, I recognized my husband in it. He'd kept no secrets.

What if I'd found pornography hidden in the back? Or maybe an envelope of secret cash? There might have been mysterious phone numbers, web addresses, or names. Instead, every item made sense. Although Nate couldn't have predicted the contents of his drawers would be listed in a book, he had nothing to hide. The contents were clean, as was his life.

Sometimes we operate as if we can hide things from God. In addition to stuff in our purses and drawers, we try to conceal the contents of our minds, a ridiculous sham. God can't be deceived, tricked, or conned. Matthew 6:6 says, "Your Father . . . sees what is done in secret." Psalm 44:21 says He even "knows the secrets of the heart."

I've asked myself, "Would I be happy with the contents of my purse or drawers being made public?" More importantly, "Am I OK with God observing my thoughts?" He says that one day everything hidden will be spotlighted, so this surely is my warning (see Luke 8:17).

As I put everything back into Nate's drawers, I was comforted to know he was exactly who I thought he was. Now, how about me?

"There is nothing concealed that will not be disclosed,
or hidden that will not be made known."
Luke 12:2

Lord, I want to live an honest life before you and others. Please show me how. Amen.

46

Best Friends Forever

One of my oldest friends is a woman I met in college. Carole and I have known each other for forty-seven years and share a camaraderie that bridges the gap between our distant homes (eight hundred miles) and our infrequent visits (every few years).

What's the glue that holds friends together long-term? Part of it is growing through life's changes simultaneously: marriage, children, mortgages, middle age. Another part is knowing each other so well that all pretense is gone. It feels good to be with someone who will stick with you, no matter what you do or say.

Many widows describe an aching isolation after their husbands die, including a strange detachment from close friends. Couple-friends drift away because the wives worry that if they invite a new widow to join them, she might feel pressured to attend the event before she's ready. One survey said a widow loses 75 percent of her friendship base in the years immediately following her husband's death.[*] It turns out widowhood is a good opportunity to see which friends are true friends.

Along with the myriad of other changes required, God may be urging us to open up to new relationships, particularly those with other widows. My friend Carole is a widow as I am, thirteen years further along. Losing our men has been the most significant event of our adult lives, and shared widowhood has served to strengthen our bond. Finding women with whom we share this experience can lead to fulfilling friendships and opportunities to help one another.

---

[*] Miriam Neff, *From One Widow to Another* (Chicago: Moody, 2009), 105.

Scripture tells us another good place to meet new friends is among women who share our faith. The psalmist said it well in Psalm 119 when he wrote, "I am a friend to all who fear you, to all who follow your precepts" (verse 63). True friends can be unlimited if you start with faith in God as your common denominator.

I often wonder about the coming friendships Scripture encourages us to ponder. In Matthew we read about Jews and Gentiles sitting together with some of the most famous characters of the Bible (8:11). If we'll be chatting over a meal with some of them, no doubt we'll be making friends with all of them. And since Paradise will be about harmony and happiness, my guess is we'll be long-term friends (*really* long-term) with everyone!

God is all about relationships, between himself and people, and also person to person. While I continue to love Carole, I'm also watching for new friends the Lord will bring. She is, too. And if we have *Him* in common, I know those friendships will literally last forever.

> *"Many will come from the east and the west,*
> *and will take their places at the feast with Abraham,*
> *Isaac and Jacob in the kingdom of heaven."*
> Matthew 8:11

Lord, please show me who my true friends are, and cause me to be a blessing to each one. Amen.

47

God Wants a Yes

The implication of being a yes-man isn't good, a yes-man being a person with no opinion of one's own. It's someone who gives in quickly and kowtows to others: "Yes, sir." "Yes, ma'm." "Whatever you say."

Although all of us hate to be pressured into giving a yes when we're really feeling a no, we all love to be on the receiving end of yeses. As my son Klaus puts it, "Green lights are better than red ones." But the ultimate yes is the one we hope to receive from God after laying out our requests. "Would you please . . . ?" we ask, hoping for His yes ASAP.

While God decides to answer us with a yes or no, is it possible *He* wants to be on the receiving end of a yes too? When He asks if we're willing to do something difficult or fight a painful battle, how do we answer?

Henry Blackaby says, "Let this be your heart's desire: 'Lord, whatever you say, my answer is yes, because that's the only worthy response to you.'"* So we're supposed to become yes-women?

As I read that statement from the comfort of my La-Z-Boy, feet up, Coke in hand, I could say, "Whatever you bring, Lord! I'll say yes!"

But when I learned that Nate had only a short time to live, it wasn't quite that easy to give an affirmative response. As time quickly slipped away and God asked if I was willing to be a widow, I didn't answer at all.

In life's battle trenches, we feel we're doing well in our faith if we go through trouble without raging at God. However, the response He longs to hear *during* our suffering is yes, even if spoken through tears.

---

* Henry Blackaby, *Experiencing Prayer with Jesus* (Sisters, OR: Multnomah, 2006), 45.

Jesus modeled it perfectly, saying essentially: "Not what I want, Father, but yes to your will for me, no matter how excruciating" (see Matthew 26:39, 42). Paul reiterated the point in 2 Corinthians 1, holding up the Father and Son as our examples: "No matter how many promises God has made, they are 'Yes' in Christ" (verse 20).

Despite my own failures, I think success is more likely if I tell the Lord how much I want to be His yes-woman. If I say yes before I've hit the suffering, then when the pain begins, my want-to is already in place. It might be only a weak, "Yes, I'll try," or "Yes, I hope so," but it will be a yes.

> *Yes, Lord, walking in the way of your laws, we wait for you;*
> *your name and renown are the desire of our hearts.*
> Isaiah 26:8

Lord, please give me a yes-infused heart that will make me quick to agree with your will for me. Amen.

48

Shaky Security

In the days following the 9/11 terrorist attacks, everything that once felt secure in our country became shaky. Peter Jennings, at the end of a TV special about that day, told all of us, "Talk to your children tonight, and assure them they'll be safe."

Nate and I had been watching the program together, and I said, "Children shouldn't be told that, because it's not true." We talked for a few minutes about the safety we do or don't have in our country and concluded the only guaranteed safety anywhere is in Christ, and that doesn't necessarily include earthly safety.

After 9/11, security measures in America drastically increased. Waiting in long airport lines became standard for flyers. Passengers were pulled aside at random and searched to make airplanes safer. Despite added rules, however, safety couldn't be guaranteed.

Recently a widow friend told me about her battle with fear after her husband died. She had never spent a night alone and was having difficulty sleeping, fearful of a break-in. Every little noise sent a chill up her spine. Sadly, though, no one can assure her a break-in will never occur. So what is she to do?

Proverbs says, "Do not let wisdom and understanding out of your sight, preserve sound judgment and discretion . . . When you lie down, you will not be afraid . . . your sleep will be sweet . . . The Lord will be at your side" (3:21–26). Wisdom understands God's promise that He'll never abandon my friend. Therefore she can picture Jesus watching over her while she sleeps, and no matter what happens, He'll partner with her through it.

My twenty-something daughter lives in Chicago and walks home from work with pepper spray in her hand. Two blocks north of her neighborhood a pair of young girls were clubbed with a baseball bat when an attacker wanted their purses. So as her mom, the only way I can sleep at night is to entrust her care to God.

We live in a world fraught with danger. Our only security comes in trusting the Lord for ultimate safety, which may not come until after we die. Nate, having left this world, is now 100 percent protected. No more airport security searches, bumps in the night, or danger in the street. He's untouchable.

The rest of us can install alarm systems or even hire armed guards to protect us, but who are we fooling? Bad things will continue to happen to good people. Although our bodies and our earthly lives will always be at risk in this shaky world, our souls can be secure in God's unshakable care. Once we truly believe this, we can rest easy.

In peace I will lie down and sleep, for you alone,
Lord, make me dwell in safety.
Psalm 4:8

Lord, when my anxiety level rises because I feel unsafe, remind me that true safety can be found only in you. Amen.

49

Comforted Inside and Out

I've given away most of Nate's clothes, but there's one piece I'm planning to keep. And wear. It's his navy blue, terrycloth bathrobe.

Nate wore this robe daily. When he was plagued by severe back pain, he couldn't wait to get out of his business suit and into the comfort of his bathrobe. Usually the transition was made immediately after our seven o'clock dinner by way of a hot soak in the tub with a few newspapers. He'd say, "One of the reasons I like this robe so much is that it's like a giant towel. It does the drying off for me."

Although there were nights during his stressful career when he'd fall into bed late at night wearing his white, long-sleeved dress shirt still buttoned at the wrists, in recent years he'd done away with all that. During his last year, he worked deliberately to reduce his escalating pain and find a measure of comfort each evening, thus the robe.

Once in a while, before the cancer diagnosis, I'd get frustrated watching him abdicate the hustle and bustle of family life in favor of undressing and heading for bed. I even grew to dislike the navy robe, which for both of us represented the end of his day. I'd say, "Are you getting ready for bed already? It's only eight o'clock!"

Now, of course, I feel bad about the implication of that question, but I hadn't understood the extent of his pain.

These days, as I wrap myself in his "giant towel," the robe brings comfort to me, too. I think about him wearing it and marvel at his lack of complaining. I know he'd smile to see me finally appreciating his robe. He'd laugh to see how it looks on me—the shoulders drooping and the belt nearly going around me twice. He'd be happy to know I've discovered there's comfort in that terrycloth.

Widow pals tell me they find soothing peace in wearing a husband's jacket, shirt, or socks. It sounds silly, especially if they didn't share their men's clothing while they were alive. But it's one of the few remaining links we widows have to our partners, and because of that, wearing their clothes brings comfort.

Scripture tells us God is a fabulous comforter. His Holy Spirit wraps himself around us, supplying deep-down warmth in those cold places where we miss our husbands. Jesus promised that when we mourn, He'll lead us out of our grief (see Matthew 5:4). One of the many ways He did that for me was by coaxing me into Nate's terrycloth robe.

Praise be to the God and Father of our Lord Jesus Christ,
the Father of compassion and the God of all comfort,
who comforts us in all our troubles.
2 Corinthians 1:3–4

Lord, I'm counting on your Spirit for my comfort and do believe you will help me. Amen.

50

Widow Blessings

Although it seems incongruous, widowhood has its perks. Lest you think I've stopped missing Nate, I haven't. I recall his face, voice, and personality every daytime hour and often into the night. But several of my widowed friends have encouraged me to count an unusual type of blessing.

For example, one afternoon I left the house on an errand-running excursion at 4:30. Around 6:30, a subconscious prompt told me it was time to head home and start supper. Nate used to walk in the door at 6:50 every weekday, and the smell of dinner cooking was a highlight he anticipated throughout his business day.

That afternoon as I pushed my cart through the grocery store's aisles, I sadly realized there was no rush. Nate wasn't on his way home, and whatever dinner I fixed would be eaten alone. The hour didn't matter. But I also realized I could finish my errands, a small thing but something my widow-experienced pals would label a blessing.

This was new for me, and it didn't sit well. Although I looked for positives during each of Nate's forty-two diagnosed cancer days, this kind of blessing-hunt seemed like betrayal. Feeling gratitude for a benefit resulting from his death seemed wrong.

Does God label these "widow blessings"? Even before answering that, I thought of another one. Nate liked listening to music, but only in the car. He thought music in a home inhibited conversation. My thinking was just the opposite, that music added an upbeat ambiance to chores, meals, entertaining, almost anything. These days I can listen to music around the clock if I choose. I'd rather have Nate back, but since I can't, I should count music as a blessing.

My guess is many widows continue in marriage patterns after theirs ends because they want life to stay the same. I read of one widow who started doing what her husband had wanted in an effort to soothe her guilt. This negates the gifts of today.

What's the proper balance between a merry widow and one who can't move out of gloom? God gives us blessings every single day, some obvious and others more subtle. Psalm 103:5 says the Lord "satisfies your desires with good things." As wives, we noticed the "good things," but as widows it's more difficult to see them. After a husband dies, we swirl in grief for months and sometimes years, but God is still pouring out blessings, even as we weep. If we look for them, our grief will ease.

After that evening of errands, I began to notice new ways God was sustaining, encouraging, and benefitting me, within my widowhood. Really! And if Nate could read the above words about music, he'd say, "Turn it up, Dear, and let music fill the house!"

Though I sit in darkness, the Lord will be my light.
Micah 7:8

Lord, please open my eyes to the widow blessings you're giving me. Amen.

Part 6

Moving Forward

51

Called to Widowhood

Every day Jack and I take a midnight walk. One frosty winter night as my boots crunched their way around multiple blocks and Jack frolicked in fresh snow, he threw himself repeatedly into the soft drifts. Rolling on his back while kicking the air with all four legs was his way of showing me how happy he was.

I hadn't dressed warmly enough and was counting the steps until we got home. By the time we reached the driveway, I was shivering but happy to finally be opening the back door. Jack, however, was disappointed and planted himself at the end of the driveway as if to say, "Let's stay out and play!"

Same facts. Two perspectives.

I often think of Nate in this regard. Although he trembled when he first heard something serious might be wrong with him, after accepting his terminal diagnosis, he became peaceful. For me it was the opposite. When I heard "pancreatic cancer," I stayed strong and was able to encourage him. But after he accepted that death was coming, I broke down often, aghast at that prospect.

Same facts. Two perspectives.

I have a choice to look at widowhood from two perspectives. I can dwell on the negatives or view it as my current calling. Depending on which perspective I take, I can either self-talk to create a "poor me" mentality or count my blessings.

Usually we think of a calling as something special, like being called to missions, teaching, or the pastorate. People are also called to singlehood, marriage, and motherhood. But widowhood? The word *widow* conjures up images of a black widow spider or dark Hollywood dramas. The widows in storybooks are described as lonely, needy outcasts. How could widowhood be a calling?

Because I've committed my life to God's leadership, I regularly ask Him to superimpose His plans over mine. I tell Him I'm willing to go through whatever He decides is best to teach me what I need to learn. If coping with widowhood is part of that, then widowhood is my calling. As extreme as that sounds, it jives with Scripture: "We know that in all things God works for the good of those who love him, who have been called according to his purpose" (Romans 8:28).

His purpose for me right now is to be a widow. Lest I despair, though, the same verse also says God is working for my good. The fact that He's working in my life at all is remarkable; that He's working for my good is extraordinary. And so I agree with what He's doing, and widowhood is where I want to be.

Same facts. Same perspective.

> *What, then, shall we say in response to these things?*
> *If God is for us, who can be against us?*
> Romans 8:31

Lord, if I'm to be content as a widow, it will have to be your doing. Please show me how this is your calling for me. Amen.

52

Shared Widowhood

Today I listened to a call-in radio interview of two widows who'd both written about their experiences, one having been alone for four years, the other eighteen months. The show was titled "The Daily Challenges of Learning to Be a Widow." The minute these two ladies came on the air, I felt a strong kinship with them, though both were strangers to me.

A caller asked about wedding rings, specifically how to know when it was time to take them off. The first widow to answer said she hadn't taken hers off yet and had begun wearing her husband's ring, too. The other said she'd taken her ring off one month after her husband's death because she wanted to look at her hand and be reminded of who was missing.

These widows then discussed the question, "What is my new place in life?" The answers varied, though they agreed on the necessity of a great deal of introspective work and the painful passing of time.

The program also tackled the question, "How much do I rearrange my life and how soon?" One call-in widow had to move out of her home immediately, because she kept thinking her husband might walk through the door he'd walked through so many times before. Of course she knew he wouldn't, but the pain of forgetting and then remembering again was a roller coaster she chose not to ride.

Many widows have e-mail addresses with their husband's name in them. They wonder, "Is it more helpful to delete his name or leave it as a comforting reminder?"

One younger widow talked of the stress of raising children alone. While that was being discussed, an older widow called to say having young children forces a widow to stay in the mainstream, make regular meals, structure sleep and wake times, and attend happy childhood functions.

During that hour my mind pictured a crowd of widows, all with different stories and responses to their dilemmas but marching forward, shoulder-to-shoulder, determination on their faces. Yet shared widowhood isn't our only source of strength. God himself stands with us in unique ways, looking out for us just as a husband would. He is intimately knowledgeable about every loss and knows our empty places, offering to fill each void. The abundant life Jesus mentions in John 10:10 is for us, too. "I have come that they may have life, and have it to the full."

When the radio program concluded, I felt much better than I had at the start. It was encouraging to know that women all over the world (245 million of them) are working to build new lives without their mates, just like I am. And if we let God help us, He'll see to it that we experience life to its fullest.

> *The Lord your God is God of gods and Lord of lords,*
> *the great God, mighty and awesome . . .*
> *He defends the cause of . . . the widow.*
> Deuteronomy 10:17–18

Lord, remind me often that I'm not alone in my widowhood. Amen.

53

Monitoring Grief

I once read a book dedicated to "the four chambers of my heart," a tribute to the author's four children. Those of us who are moms *get* that. Our heartfelt love would throw us in front of a truck if it meant sparing our children pain, and we hurt deeply as we watch them grieve for their fathers.

Several parents in the Bible agonized while watching their children suffer, but the most dramatic case was Mary, Jesus' mother. Although she knew from the beginning her son would be unusual, Gabriel had given her only the good news: He'd be the Son of the Most High, a king on David's throne, a holy child, the Son of God.

Eight days after Jesus' birth, she heard the bad news. While in the temple consecrating Jesus to the Lord, she was told He'd eventually bring major mother heartbreak: "This child is destined to cause the falling and rising of many in Israel, and to be a sign that will be spoken against . . . And a sword will pierce your own soul too" (Luke 2:34–35).

As Jesus grew, assuredly a delightful child, Mary must have watched for those negatives, wondering how such intense pain could possibly come through this exceptional son. Years later she watched Him on the cross and was, indeed, stabbed in her mother-heart. Witnessing her son's agony without being able to diminish it was the greatest pain she'd ever know. (Forgive me as I hold back about the unmitigated anguish Jesus experienced.)

I thought about Mary as I watched my own children grieve, feeling a bond with her. The Bible doesn't describe her emotions, but we know she didn't try to interfere or lessen Jesus' suffering. Then one day God added to my thoughts about her. "She wasn't the only parent suffering while watching," He whispered. "I was too."

Although human moms can't usually ease their children's grief, God could have aborted every bit of His Son's agony. Yet He didn't. He let it continue, because something immensely valuable was going to come from it. Although my children's suffering can't compare to Mary's and certainly not to God's, the Lord convinced me He was going to make their grief-stricken days count for something valuable, too.

It's as if He said, "Your children are missing their father, but I'm coaxing them to come closer to me and am developing compassion within them, among many other things. I won't waste an ounce of their sadness."

Suddenly, my inability to lighten their loads took on a new dimension. God didn't figuratively "throw himself in front of the truck" for Jesus, and neither did Mary. So I needed to stand back, too, and let the Father bring value from their grief.

> *We know that God is greater than our hearts,*
> *and he knows everything.*
> 1 John 3:20

Lord, when my heart aches watching my children suffer, remind me that you'll bring good from their sorrow. Amen.

54

Staying in the Race

It's a miracle my car hasn't run out of gas since Nate died. I didn't fill my own tank for decades, because he always did it for me, which meant he had to have my gas gauge on his mind every day. He had to remember to get in my car and check it, and then arrange a time to drive to the station for a fill-up. He continued serving me in this way even after his back pain made sitting difficult.

In the months since he's been gone, my Toyota's gas gauge has been dangerously close to resting on the "E" pin repeatedly, and only the flashing light on my dashboard has rescued me. Every time I stand at the pump refueling, I miss my husband.

The loving act of gassing-up a wife's car isn't mentioned in the Bible's love chapter (1 Corinthians 13), but it's there between the lines. Cars need gas, and I needed Nate, in many more ways than just servicing my car. Getting used to widowhood means learning to move forward without my husband, and that results in running close to empty once in a while.

Living life is much like being in a race. As widows we're still in it but feel like we've come to a massive roadblock. Our preferred course and the route we formerly knew has been altered, making us want to drop out of the race completely. We feel we've lost our way and don't know where to turn.

But Scripture picks up on the race analogy, and like it or not, all of us are in it. "Let us run with perseverance the race marked out for us" (Hebrews 12:1). Accepting widowhood means accepting that God has "marked out" a new course for us. And because He wants us all to reach the finish line, we can be sure He'll show us how to get there.

Several of my widow friends have actually picked up the pace since their men died, tackling jobs they wouldn't have been inclined to do while married. They didn't ask for these new assignments, but God has offered them. So they've chosen not to view them as second-best because they're widows, but as positive purposes for their lives. And as they've said yes to this rerouting, the Lord has fueled their efforts.

Sometimes we feel lost without our men, but we ought never to feel stuck behind a barricade or speed bump to such an extent that we can't go on. Our husbands have finished their races, but we haven't, and until we do, God has specifically chosen roads He wants us to travel. And just as Nate faithfully filled my gas tank, the Lord will faithfully fuel us to keep moving forward, because He wants all of us to reach the finish line in victory.

> *The Lord blessed the latter part of Job's life*
> *more than the former part.*
> Job 42:12

Lord, when I feel I can't run this new race you've marked out for me, fill me with perseverance and the energy to keep going. Amen.

55

Worth the Wait

Nate had enough numbers savvy for both of us, which was good, since I had none. Before he got sick, we talked about how I would handle things if anything ever happened to him. He explained the necessary tasks in simple terms, but not much of it stuck.

Once cancer arrived, there was little time to work on paperwork, and when he died quickly, chaos awaited. Most widows experience something similar, and I'm thankful God sends helpers to rescue us. However, I remember one miserable day when I tried to get a tax question answered. I spent three hours in line at the IRS.

When I arrived on the twenty-fourth floor of the office building, a uniformed official directed me to a line that stretched far down a long hallway. Trudging to the end, I asked the guy in front of me how long he'd been waiting. "Two hours. So far."

Each new arrival got the same treatment. "Where do I go to get an answer to a tax question?"

"Right there," the official would say, pointing a finger to the line.

As we inched forward, the clock ticked toward closing time, making all of us edgy. Finally a tax expert appeared in the hall. "We won't get to any of you people today," she said, sweeping her hand down the length of the line. Waiters groaned in unison, but I rejoiced to be one of only three who were told to keep waiting. Sadly, though, when my turn finally came, help didn't. The tax man directed me to a different office with a new line to stand in, on another day.

Most of us dislike waiting, and my miserable wait in the tax line is an example of why. God knows it's difficult for us but asks us to wait anyway. Scripture says, "Be still before the Lord and wait patiently for him" (Psalm 37:7). Because we're easily frustrated by having to wait in line (or wait for anything, for that matter), we're liable to feel the same irritation with God while waiting for Him to act on our behalf.

Just as those in the tax line had no idea how long the wait would be, the Lord doesn't let us know how long our grieving will last. Just as the officials on the twenty-fourth floor had all the power, God is sovereign over the events of our lives. And just as the authorities kept us from looking into the room where help was located, God keeps us from seeing into our futures.

Although He often asks us to wait, He has important reasons. When the time is right, He satisfies us with answers to our questions. Meanwhile, we can line up with the psalmist who says, "I wait for the Lord, my whole being waits, and in his word I put my hope" (Psalm 130:5).

Since ancient times no one has heard,
no ear has perceived, no eye has seen any God besides you,
who acts on behalf of those who wait for him.
Isaiah 64:4

Lord, increase my patience to wait for your rescue. Amen.

56

Travel Turmoil

Going on a trip was always exciting, starting with the inception of a travel idea through the loading of the suitcases. Nate gathered maps, managed rides to the airport, and kept track of plane tickets. He informed the rest of the family of our whereabouts and did the worrying for both of us. We enjoyed coffee together while waiting at the gate, and because he was a white-knuckle flier, he distracted himself by getting acquainted with other passengers.

Now that he's gone, I still travel a little, but some of the sparkle has disappeared, and when it comes time to return home, gear-shifting is difficult. The minute I step in the door, I'm poked with exclamation points from all directions. The mail shouts, "Pay these bills! Respond to these letters!"

The refrigerator screams, "Your milk is sour! Your sandwich meat has expired!" The dishwasher shouts, "Unload me!" Even the wall calendar hollers with commitments made before I left.

It's not easy to shift gears, even after plenty of practice. When we were kids, fall brought a shift in classrooms. College was a shift in home and lifestyle, marriage a shift from single to double. Parenthood forced major changes, followed by reversing the process for an empty nest.

But widowhood has been the most challenging shift of all, a change the equivalent of returning from a thousand trips. My mind frequently swirls in confusion or churns over unpleasant surprises. Thankfully I can go to the One who's never been confused or surprised by anything.

Scripture gives us a word picture to explain how remarkable this is: "The Father . . . does not change like shifting shadows" (James 1:17). Our human shadows move dramatically as the sun crosses the sky, starting out long, becoming short, and returning to long again. Shadows angle left or right, depending on the position of the sun, and they tilt according to our movement.

God isn't like that. His shadow never shifts, because He doesn't have one. He's everywhere, always, in all capacities. While we struggle with gear-shifting, He's constant and sure, a rock of stability to the life changes we have to make continually. As we go from one circumstance to another, His reality stays the same.

This is good news for widows. While we're adjusting to our new role and trying to cope with changes in every life category, we can lean hard on a God who's never had to gear-shift, not for any reason. He doesn't pack or unpack, because He doesn't travel. He's already everywhere.

When I return from a trip and feel alone, attacked by exclamation points demanding my attention, I can look for help in my home and find it quickly, because He's already there.

I am with you and will watch over you wherever you go,
and I will bring you back.
Genesis 28:15

Lord, I'm so glad you never change. As I travel through widowhood, please help me with this very difficult gear-shift. Amen.

57

Good Times

One of my favorite singers, Eydie Gorme, sang a song so thought-provoking that several years ago I wrote out the lyrics and filed them in a manila folder under "Time," which was the name of the tune.*

She sang, "Back when I was young and summer was forever, 'good' was your first name."

For most young couples, good times fill the youthful years, along with hope for a happy future. I remember the fun Nate and I had as newlyweds, playing house while he finished law school and I taught first grade. Although we had little possessions or money, we had priceless good times together.

Then the clock began to race, ticking even as we slept. Nate graduated, we moved, he became a lawyer, and I became a stay-at-home mommy. Seven children were born, grew up, went to college, and moved away. We had weddings, then grandchildren, and in what seemed like one quick minute, time ended, at least for Nate. My time as his wife ended, too.

Eydie sang, "Time, when did you begin trading your tomorrows for worn out just-todays?"

When I'd been a widow for three months, I remember sitting in a chair at twilight, my hands in my lap, doing absolutely nothing but listening to the tick-tock of a wall clock. Immobilized by sorrow, all I could do was listen to time slipping away. Grief had exhausted me, and life had become a series of "worn out just-todays."

---

* Eydie Gorme, vocal performance of "Time," by Roger Nichols and Paul Williams, on *Tonight I'll Say a Prayer*, RCA Victor, LSP-4303, 1970.

Scripture says, "When times are good, be happy; but when times are bad, consider this: God has made the one as well as the other" (Ecclesiastes 7:14). With this verse the Lord reminded me I was in His care during bad times as well as good. My grieving was no less important to Him than my laughter, and that brought me comfort.

When Nate died, I was convinced life could never be good again. Sure, there would be new relationships and experiences, but they were bound to fall short of how it would have been with him there to share in them. I've since learned that because God holds every passing minute in His hands, He can (and does) surprise us with good times when we least expect them. Though I know my remaining years will be different than I anticipated because Nate is gone, God has shown me that different doesn't always equate to bad.

Eydie sang, "Time, you rolled into years, years that left me walking, when you began to fly."

Time is definitely flying, and I may be walking rather than running, but sometimes a long walk can turn out to be a really good time.

> *The race is not to the swift or the battle to the strong . . .*
> *but time and chance happen to them all.*
> Ecclesiastes 9:11

Lord, although today I might feel too sad to believe that good times are coming, please teach me to anticipate a brighter tomorrow. Amen.

58

The Bad in Good-bye

When I was a child, good-byes were important. Mom always made a big deal of saying good-bye to Dad as he headed out the door each morning, kissing and hugging him until he finally said, "All right, that's enough."

After we were grown, married, and visiting "back home," Mom and Dad would stand in their driveway waving us off until we were out of sight. Then, as an elderly widow, Mom would come over for dinner each week, after which it was our turn to stand in the driveway waving to her.

Nate and I also said countless good-byes to our seven children as they left home for college, mission trips, or marriage, most of our farewells once again in the driveway, waving until they disappeared. Good-byes are important, because we never know which one will be the last.

The hardest good-byes take place in the moments when someone is dying. These separations are emotionally charged, because unlike the others, we *know* it will be the last. After Nate died, it occurred to me that someday I'll be on a deathbed too, saying good-bye to those gathered around me, exactly as we did with him.

Since I've become a widow, every good-bye seems more potent and somehow sadder. Even waving to someone I plan to see in a week's time is cause for tearing up, because prominent in my mind is the true statement, "You never know . . ."

Scripture says, "People are destined to die" (Hebrews 9:27), so we're in for many upsetting good-byes. We widows have already experienced one of the most difficult.

The Bible is dotted with significant good-byes, but the hardest must have been in relation to Jesus. As He was being arrested, all of His disciples, with the exception of John, apparently threw away their opportunities for loving farewells. Figuratively speaking, they could have "stood in the driveway" and waved their love and prayer support to Him as He trudged toward Calvary. Instead they snuck away.

But then there was Jesus' mother. She stuck with Him until the end, enduring excruciating emotional pain to breathe her good-bye as He surrendered His life.

Good-byes usually aren't so good. I've thought of the difficult good-bye that must have taken place between the Father and Son when Jesus departed heaven to become a human with all the resulting limitations. That separation lasted thirty-three years and included tremendous agony for both of them. Eventually, though, they were reunited, and no future good-byes were on their schedules.

The rest of us will also get to live that no-more-good-byes existence one day. After we've gone to heaven, we'll be reunited with our loved ones, and amazingly, we'll get to meet Jesus. Once we've taken up residence with Him, "good-bye" will never be spoken again.

> *"No one has ever gone to heaven and returned."*
> John 3:13 (NLT)

Lord, keep me from self-pity and sadness during good-byes, and remind me that you will always be close. Amen.

59

Proper Priorities

Nate and I raised our family in a hundred-year-old farmhouse, the last of its kind in our small suburb northwest of Chicago. When it came time to downsize, we moved 110 miles to a much smaller home we'd used as a summer cottage. Although the house hadn't been updated since the sixties, we loved its small size, quiet neighborhood, and diminished responsibilities.

After moving in June, we talked about which refurbishing project to tackle first, deciding we'd pull up the living room carpet. After forty years it was stained and rumpled, and we wanted to expose the oak flooring beneath it. "In the fall," Nate said, "after we get unpacked and settled."

But when fall came, cancer came, too. Renovations fell on the priority list while more important things rose: doctor appointments, radiation treatments, trips to the Chicago hospital, and pharmacy visits. Above all of that was family time with Nate, and trumping everything was meeting our desperate need for God's help.

Prayer became a necessity rather than an option, both privately and together. We craved God's opinion of what we should think, say, and do. Bibles remained open throughout the house, and every conversation ended on scriptural topics. Because we were in crisis mode, these became our new priorities.

Jesus says, "Whoever loses their life for my sake will find it" (Matthew 10:39). Losing one priority list to another that's not of our choosing can be frustrating and frightening. But losing our choices to God's choices can give fresh meaning to our days. This is especially true after our own plans go askew. It's then that God's priorities will make the most sense.

After Nate died, our crisis priorities had to be rearranged again. Although renovation pushed its way back up the list and we did rip up the living room carpet, home improvement projects now lacked urgency. What remained on top was talking to God, receiving counsel from Him, and leaning on Him as we began our grieving. The need for His full-time leadership became acute once our earthly leader was gone.

Life is all about setting priorities. We write them down and obey our lists. But when a crisis hits, existing priorities are tossed aside and more important ones take their places. Maybe the reason God allows trouble is because circumstances beyond our control make us rush to Him in dependency.

The trick, then, is figuring out how to keep a crisis priority list in place after the crisis has passed. Maybe we should just ask God to write it for us in the first place. Then when He rearranges it, it'll still be in the best order.

We spend our years as a tale that is told . . . Teach us to number
our days, that we may apply our hearts unto wisdom.
Psalm 90:9–12 (KJV)

Lord, show me how to keep you as my number-one priority. Amen.

60

A Lonely One

A popular song in the late sixties was titled "One": "One is the loneliest number that you'll ever do. One is the loneliest number, worse than two."*

During these last months I've worked hard at making a life for one rather than many, the reversal of a forty-year practice. Big families are all about multiple bedrooms, many chairs squeezed around the supper table, and a whole fleet of rattletrap cars in the driveway, but now I'm in a nearly empty house.

It isn't all bad. It's just that our empty nest wasn't supposed to be quite this empty. Today as I chose a small saucepan in which to make oatmeal, I had to smile at how silly it looked on the burner where much larger cookware usually sat. This pan would have fit right in with a little girl's kitchen play set, but now, it was the right size for just me.

Two things came to mind, both encouraging. First, it was God who put me in this new life of "one," and second, I suspect He's readying me for something else. In Nate's case, not knowing what was coming was a good thing, because his future held great physical pain followed by an "early" death. But what about me?

Taking a lesson from his circumstances and applying it to my life of "one," I must acknowledge that I don't need to know what's ahead. It's actually best if I don't, because sometimes God intentionally puts us in a lonely place for a time. Even Jesus found that loneliness wasn't

---

* Harry Nilsson, "One," recorded November 8, 1967, on *Aerial Ballet*, produced by Rick Jarrard, RCA, 1968.

always bad, and sometimes He initiated it. Luke 5:16 says, "Jesus often withdrew to lonely places and prayed."

Once I accept that being alone and even lonely might be God's intention for a while, I can relax in my very empty nest and make friends with a tiny saucepan. And instead of the song "One," I'm going to dwell on the chorus of another tune popular at that same time, "Known Only to Him": "I know not what the future holds, but I know who holds the future."*

This line might seem sentimental, but its principle is profound: I need to entrust my future to the One who already knows its secrets. That way, I can know that what looks uncertain to me is secure with God, no matter what happens, whether I'm in a crowd or in my kitchen cooking in a tiny saucepan just for me.

I am convinced that neither death nor life . . . nor anything else in all creation, will be able to separate us from the love of God that is in Christ Jesus our Lord.
Romans 8:38–39

Lord, as I adjust to my new life of "one," please help me look for you and your purposes in the lonely moments. Bring contentment as I trust you with whatever is ahead. Amen.

---

* Don Gibson, vocal performance of "Known Only to Him," by Stuart Hamblen, Warner Chappell Music, 1952.

Conclusion

As you come to the end of these devotions, my hope is that you've been gently moving into a new confidence about your future. You are precious to the Lord, and He has His eye on you every minute. Even during the night when your weeping is keeping you awake, God is there beside you, tenderly counting your tears and reaching out to you in love. He longs to share the weight of your grief and hopes you'll take advantage of His offer (see Psalm 9:9; 32:7; Matthew 11:28–30). Day by day He'll show you that you can lead a fulfilling and purposeful life.

I also hope that you will visit my website, www.GettingThrough This.com. There you will find encouragement to keep moving forward. Each post highlights two things: God can get us through our difficulties, and He can put solid ground beneath our feet.

Margaret

Acknowledgments

In the process of writing this book, I made new friends at Discovery House Publishers. Carol Holquist was several months ahead of me into widowhood when we first talked, and an immediate "click" resulted from our common emotions and experiences. Her encouragement to write something helpful to widows was the genesis of this book. Thank you, Carol, for taking a chance on me. When I pray for my widowed friends, I'm praying for you.

Miranda Gardner had the monumental task of tutoring me through the many stages of the editorial process, and because of her abundant patience with my endless questions, I learned a great deal and had a delightful time doing it. Thank you, Miranda, for my new education in how to pull a book together. May God bless you abundantly for your kindness to this very green author.

To the many other members of the Discovery House team who put their expert touches on this work, I thank you abundantly and stand amazed at how many skilled hands it takes to turn out one book.

And to my hard-working prayer team, thank you for being as excited about this project as I have been. You've followed God's lead and I've followed you, learning from your example of faithfulness in prayer. Because of your work behind the scenes, His influence is on every page. Thank you, especially, for lifting up the widows who will read this book. As a result, I'm confident the Lord began working in their lives well ahead of time, even preparing some for widowhood before they got there.

You're the best! "I thank my God every time I remember you. In all my prayers for all of you, I always pray with joy . . ." (Philippians 1:3–5).

Adam Curington
Barb Karnath
Birgitta Nyman
Carole Hawkinson
Carolyn Thompson
Cathy Richardson
Connie Schambach
Debbe Baker
Gaye Swaback
Hans Nyman
Jan Rode
Jan Johnson
Joy Satre
Judy Johnson
Julia Lever
Julie Erickson
Junior McGarrahan
Katy Nyman
Klaus Nyman
Lars Nyman
LeeAnn Bennett
Linda Miller

Linnea Curington
Louisa Nyman
Lynn Hammond
Marge Bryant
Maria Pietrini
Mary Gustavson
Mary Jo Rust
Mary Lou Hess
Mary Martin
Mary Peterson
Miriam Neff
Nancy Guidone
Nelson Nyman
Pam Krause
Pat Anderson
Pat D'Agostino
Rebecca Lutzer
Gloria Ryan
Sue Kerr
Susan Eriksson
Terry Davis

Note to the Reader

The publisher invites you to share your response to the message of this book by writing Discovery House Publishers, P.O. Box 3566, Grand Rapids, MI 49501, U.S.A. For information about other Discovery House books, music, videos, or DVDs, contact us at the same address or call 1-800-653-8333. Find us on the Internet at http://www.dhp.org/ or send e-mail to books@dhp.org.

About the Author

When I was a child, I prayed I could one day write books for a living and actually started one at age twelve. Although I pursued writing through college and graduate school, marrying Nate in 1969 and having seven children changed my story line significantly.

Nate's story line veered from his original plan, too. A Chicago lawyer, he found his greatest job satisfaction in the real estate world of limited partnerships. But in 1986, when the government changed the tax code without warning investors, his thriving business and our income went over a financial cliff, taking us plus seventy employees down to zero. We had six children at the time.

Yet the greatest threat to our marriage and family came in 2009 when we learned of Nate's fatal cancer. We had only forty-two days from diagnosis to death, and as I write this, we're still in the process of finding firm footing. But God has never left us and has always provided ways to cope and reasons for hope.

Our children, now grown, have been a source of extreme joy to Nate and me. And since his death, they've lovingly cared for me in my widowhood while simultaneously grieving the loss of their "Papa." Each of them continues to be an example of putting the needs of another ahead of their own, and my gratitude is unbounded. I learn from them daily.

As for the book you hold in your hand, it's God's answer to the prayers of a twelve-year-old girl who always wanted to be a writer. Fifty-four years elapsed between my first attempt and this one, but if it hadn't been for those intervening years, I wouldn't have had much to write. Adjusting to widowhood in partnership with pen and ink has kept me close to Nate in thought, a meaningful process for me. And as these pages prove, when Nate departed, God stepped into his place.